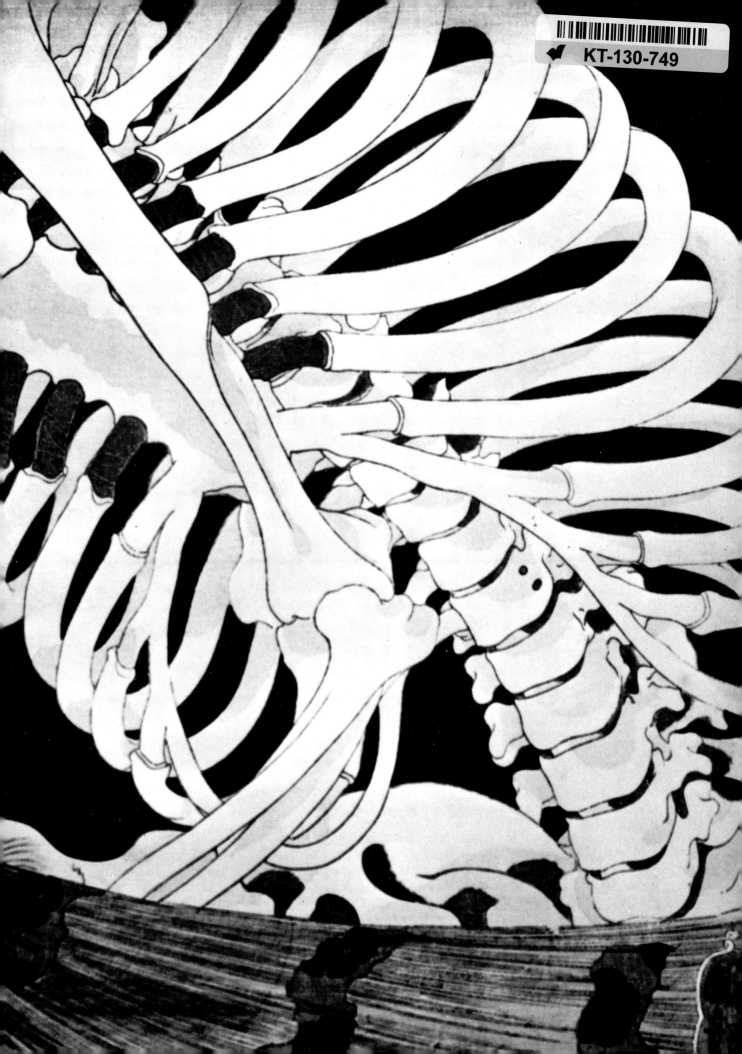

JAPANESE MYTHOLOGY

H. F. W. in love and thankfulness

JAPANESE MYTHOLOGY

JULIET PIGGOTT

PAUL HAMLYN
LONDON NEW YORK SYDNEY TORONTO

Colour Plates
Frontispiece:

Spirits of the pine tree. The two pine trees and their spirits, Jo and
Uba, sweeping the pine needles with besom and rake personify old
age and married fidelity. Both the tortoises and the storks are also
symbols of old age. The tortoises with tails of weeds are known as
Minogame. Print by Shunsen. Victoria and Albert Museum.

The Hamlyn Publishing Group Limited
London New York Sydney Toronto
Hamlyn House, Feltham, Middlesex, England

Copyright © Juliet Piggott 1969
SBN 600 021 130
All rights reserved
Printed in Italy by O.G.A.M. Verona

CONTENTS

Miss Olive Jarvis helped me with this book in a manner which is typical of her, and I do not refer only to her ability to spell. Her understanding and serenity while I was researching, writing and typing helped me in a way which those who know her will understand. And there are three families to whom I am indebted for encouragement and knowledge given, and for books and, in one case even a study, lent. They are the Blackers, the Crowes and the Storrys. All of them, like Miss Jarvis, have given friendship to me and mine around the world for more than one generation. For this my personal gratitude is deep. J. E. J. P.

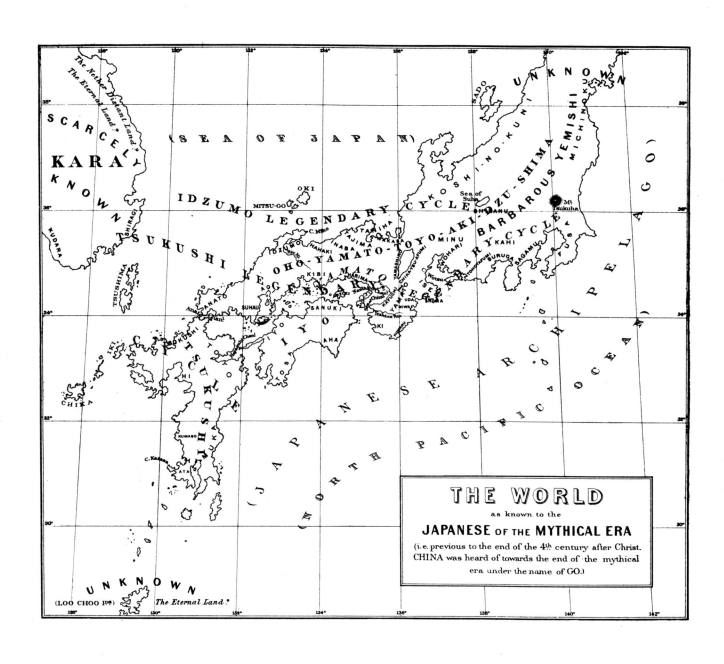

THE COUNTRY AND ITS CREATION

お板
七里ヶ濵
風波

第二三十六景

Fujiyama, the sacred mountain of Japan, has inspired countless artists. It is the goal of pilgrims and several legends centre on it. Its last major eruption was in 1707. By Hiroshige.

Perhaps nowhere else in the world are the indigenous legends so deeply embedded in the minds of the people as they are in Japan. The well known tales of gods, goddesses, heroes, and talking animals are repeated in books, in drama and within the family. Still they are told, as all good stories should be, and as they were originally, by word of mouth, for Japan is a country of myths, legends, folk tales and folk lore.

It may well be that the reason for the repetition and abundance of these stories is connected with the extremely variegated topography. Japan proper now consists of four islands: Hokkaido (formerly called Yezo) in the north; Honshu (the main island) with its six major cities including Tokyo, Kobe, Yokohama and Hiroshima; Shikoku, separated from Honshu to the south-west by the Inland Sea; and Kyushu, further west and south, whose major city is Nagasaki. The archipelago also contains a host of smaller

Right: Izanagi and Izanami of the early Shinto pantheon watch a wagtail and from it and its mate learn how they are to create offspring. Their progeny include the islands of Japan and a host of deities.

The Byodo-in at Uji, a few miles from Kyoto, dates from the middle of the eleventh century, when the original villa was converted into a Buddhist monastery and temple. The main hall, completed in 1053, represents the mythological phoenix, the outer structures being its wings and the rear its tail. Two bronze phoenixes surmount the edifice.

islands, some no bigger than a protrusion of rock from the sea. The whole forms a thousand mile semicircle. The climate of this island empire set in the north-western Pacific ranges from the semi-tropical of the south to the harsh and bitter winters of the north. It is affected not only by latitude but by the warm Japan Current on the Pacific east coast of Honshu and the cold Okhotsk Current in the Sea of Japan to the west. It is a country of mountain peaks and ranges, a volcanic land of waterfalls, lakes, hot springs and earthquakes, of typhoons and tidal waves. It is a land with swift clear rivers and an abundance of foliage ranging from the deep green of the cryptomeria through the delicate blossoms of the cherry and peach to the golden and scarlet glories of the autumn maples.

The Shinto religion also encouraged the proliferation of stories.

This religion, from which all true Japanese mythology springs, accepts that every natural thing, be it a man, a volcano, or a plum tree, has, in varying degrees of intensity, a *kami* or spirit. Some parts of the vegetable and animal kingdoms are believed to have emanated from or to be descendants of the deities. The country itself and its flora and fauna surely played a considerable part in this aspect of Japanese mythology and folk lore.

Japan went through a long period of self-imposed seclusion from the rest of the world. Moreover, in a land where river transport is seldom used – the rivers are generally shallow and swift with many waterfalls – the people have tended to remain in their own islands or areas. And while the Japanese are inveterate sightseers abroad, their appreciation of their own country's scenic beauties is coupled with a patriotism peculiar to the Japanese.

The temples and shrines, both Shinto and Buddhist, seem to merge into the wooded, hilly country and nowhere is there a better example of this than the temple area at Nikko, some hundred miles north of Tokyo, where the Tokugawa shoguns are buried. The Japanese word *kekko* means beautiful, and there can be few foreign travellers in Japan who have not heard the proverb, 'One must not say *kekko* until one has seen Nikko.'

Perhaps because of this seclusion and awareness of natural surroundings, the majority of legends are local, connected with a specific area or with a feature of it. For example, several legends have arisen around Mt Fuji. It is said to have been formed during a great earthquake in 286 B.C. The earthquake also caused the ground to open, as happened as recently as 1923 when Yokohama and most of Tokyo were destroyed. Lake Biwa (*biwa* is a musical instrument shaped like a lute or mandolin) was formed in what used to be called Omi Province in south-west Honshu. In Omi there also arose from the Underworld a small hill called Migami, similar in shape to Fuji. Fuji has from time immemorial been a sacred mountain and it is said that in olden times natives from Omi could climb her after only seven days of purification instead of the usual hundred, on account of the likeness of their Migami to the mountain of their pilgrimage.

Fuji is generally believed to be a female. She is the highest mountain in Japan. It is said that at one time Mt Haku, a male, towered above her. The Buddha Amida was asked to decide which peak was in fact the higher. He ran a pipe from the top of Haku to the top of Fuji and poured water into it. The water flowed down to Fuji's peak and she, in her rage at the proven result of the contest, beat Haku about the head. By cracking his skull into eight parts, she reduced his height and also caused Mt Haku's eight peaks. This tale is told of other mountains in the country and doubtless modern knowledge of measuring mountain heights has caused the locale of the myth to be changed from time to time.

The origin of the Japanese people is obscure, but it is generally accepted that the Ainu, who now inhabit Hokkaido, were the aborigines. In myths and stories they are often referred to as the Barbarians. Invaders drove the Ainu north and it is probable that these tribes came from the mainland of Asia via the Korean peninsula. It is no part of this book to discuss the various modern theories of population and migration, for Japanese mythology provides its own story of the creation of Japan and her population. It was believed, however, in certain quarters at the end of the last century that the Japanese were one of the lost tribes of Israel. The enthusiasts of this 'myth' suspected the tribe to be that of Benjamin.

Creation myths

A great carp asleep under the sea who had, in waking, thrashed the waters causing both tidal waves and the appearance of the islands of Japan, is a popular tale among the young. But the usual mythological story of the creation of the empire runs very differently and is taken from the oldest records. The origin of these records is described in the following chapter.

Izanagi and Izanami

Out of the primeval oily ocean mass, a reed-like substance emerged. This became a deity, and at the same time two other divine creatures, male and female, came into being. Little is told of this original trio, but they did produce generations of gods and goddesses in their celestial land, and after a period of unmeasured time a pair of gods were finally created called Izanagi and Izanami. Their names in translation are 'Male-who-invites' and 'Female-who-invites' respectively. They came down from their heaven to the oily mass by a bridge, generally accepted to have been a rainbow. Izanagi disturbed the primeval ocean with his spear and the drops from its tip congealed and, in falling, formed the island of Ono-koro or 'self-

coagulating.' This is one of the earliest suggestions of phallicism in Japanese mythology.

Although Izanagi and Izanami were supposedly brother and sister, they married on Ono-koro. They learned the art of love-making by watching a pair of wagtails, and these water birds are still associated with the couple. Even the god of Scarecrows cannot frighten wagtails, a blessing given the birds at their creation.

Among the offspring of Izanagi and Izanami were geographical landmarks, including the rest of the Japanese islands, waterfalls, and mountains, trees, herbs and the wind. The wind completed the creation of Japan, for he it was who blew away the hazy mists and revealed the scattered islands for the first time. The first child of the two gods was miscarried (supposedly through a misdemeanour on Izanami's part at the marriage ceremony) and this jellyfish-like creature was, not surprisingly, put into the sea.

All their other children survived. The last to be born after the string of islands had been formed and populated was the cause of his mother's death. He was the god of fire. After his birth, Izanami became ill with a burning fever which finally killed her. She went to the Underworld – Yomi, the Land of Gloom – but Izanagi followed her there in spite of her protests. She chased him, aided by hideous female spirits, in order to punish him for pursuing her, but he just managed to escape back to the world. At the entrance of Yomi, she screamed after him that in revenge she would denude the world of its inhabitants by destroying a thousand daily. However, Izanagi replied that he would create fifteen hundred each day.

In this story not only did the pair, through their marriage and progeny, establish the pattern of nature for all time, but through their 'divorce' they created mortal life and death.

Izanagi kept his word, and after undergoing a ritual purification to wash away the effects of his descent into the Underworld, he gave birth to the Sun goddess, the Moon god and to Susano the Storm god. In one version, it is told that these three were created from Izanagi's eyes.

Amaterasu, the Sun goddess

Many myths explain natural phenomena. The Sun and Moon brother and sister have an uneasy relationship and sit in their celestial land which is curiously like Japan in structure, with their backs to one another: hence day and night. The Sun goddess, Amaterasu, is looked upon as the deity from whom the imperial family is descended. Of the host of stories connected with her, one of the best known is that of her withdrawal into a cave. Amaterasu and Susano were not friends. As the Storm God, he was a troublesome character. He once visited her domain on the pretext of making amends for previous unruly behaviour. Instead he destroyed her rice fields by loosing piebald colts among them and generally desecrated much of her property. She retaliated by retiring into a cave, thus darkening the whole world. Amaterasu did not come out until a goddess, encouraged by a multitude of minor gods and goddesses, all making a great uproar the while, performed a dance which some describe as merry and others as obscene, outside the cave. Overcome by curiosity, Amaterasu emerged and in doing so saw her reflection in a mirror which the gods had fashioned and hung on a tree while she was in hiding. This was the first mirror and it forms a part of the imperial regalia of Japan. Since the cave episode, the world has experienced normal day and night.

Susano, the Storm god

Susano, however, is not entirely limited to his role as Storm god. His name has been translated as 'Swift-Impetuous-Deity' and

The Country and its Creation

'The Impetuous Male.' He was banished from Amaterasu's celestial country and went to the Province of Izumo on the coast of the Sea of Japan in Honshu. From there he was said to have planted forests on the coasts of Korea from the hairs of his beard, and because of this he is associated with forests in general. He is depicted as being heavily bearded and is perhaps connected with the hairy Ainu.

Susano and his progeny are also associated with Izumo. His grandson, Omi-tsu-nu, on coming into his inheritance, wanted to extend the territory of the province. He changed the coastline to its present shape by dragging towards him pieces of land from Korea and also certain islands off the Izumo coast by means of ropes connected to a mountain. These portions of land, when all joined together, formed the peninsula in the north of Izumo. The last

Amaterasu, the Sun goddess, is lured out of her cave, where she had withdrawn following her younger brother's spoliation of her property, by the dancing of the gods and goddesses outside. Note the Sacred Mirror and Jewels hanging on the sakaki tree on the right of the picture. After this episode normal day and night returned to the world.

Far right: the Wedded Rocks at Futami. The torii is a Shinto one. The twisted straw ropes here symbolise marriage, but in many Shinto shines they are used to ward off both evil spirits and infection.

Bottom right: Buddhist sculptures are often seen by the roads in country districts. This photograph was taken near Nara.

rope used in this complicated operation was tied to Mt Taisen, and Yomi beach, which lies at its foot, is said to be the remains of it.

Many other stories are told about Susano in good or evil guise. One of the most popular tells how he killed an eight-headed dragon in Izumo. He did this by making it drunk with eight bowls of *sake*, the Japanese alcoholic drink made from distilled rice. In one version the sake is poisoned. Susano used his courage and cunning to kill the dragon in order to rescue a minor goddess, a girl, whose many sisters had been eaten in turn annually by the dragon. The heroine in the story was the last surviving daughter of the family and as could be expected, she married Susano. Their children pass into mythical history and beyond.

In the tail of the dead dragon, Susano found the sword which is another part of the imperial regalia. During one of the infrequent periods when he and his sister were amiably disposed towards one another he gave it to Amaterasu. In return she gave him some of her jewels, which form the third part of the regalia. On another occasion she gave him other jewels which he used as hail and lightning in his capacity of Storm god.

Izumo province provides the setting for most of the earliest myths, but other parts of Japan have theirs too. One such myth explains why there are no foxes on the island of Shikoku. After the time of the Buddhist saint, Kobo Daishi (774-835 A.D.), no story set there has a fox in it, for he was supposed to have purged the island of the animals by driving them into the sea. The animal stories of Shikoku have badgers, cats or dogs in place of the mischievous or evil fox.

Trees and rocks

All over Japan one hears stories of trees which have a peculiar or
beautiful shape. One pair of twisted and entwined pines is supposed
to be a pair of lovers. The boy and girl wandered far from their
village and as night fell, were afraid to return and face either the
displeasure of their families or the taunts of their friends. All night
they embraced and talked of their love, and when morning broke
they had been transformed into these pine trees. Another pair of pines
is said to be a devoted couple who died at the same time. These
trees represent fidelity as well as the more usual prosperous old age.

In Kyushu on the coast of Matsura there is a rock known as the Rock
of Sayo-hime. Like so many curiously shaped rock formations, it
has its story. Sayo-hime was the wife of an official whose duties

Raiko, more commonly known as Yorimitsu, the Minamoto hero of legend, who with his four lieutenants battled with oni, ghosts and other fabulous creatures. Here they attack a demon in human form and a bull. Print by Kuniyoshi. Victoria and Albert Museum.

18

took him to China. In ancient times Matsura was the port for the Asian mainland. She stood waving him good-bye long after his ship had disappeared, until eventually her body turned into the rock bearing her name.

Uke-mochi

Just as the physical formation of the volcanic islands provide stories or myths, so do their crops. The Moon god was sent down to Earth by his elder sister, Amaterasu, to see that the Food deity, Uke-mochi, was performing her duties. In order to entertain this higher being, since Amaterasu and her two brothers took precedence over other deities, Uke-mochi opened her mouth while facing the fields and boiled rice streamed from it. When she faced the sea, fish and edible seaweed were regurgitated, and when she faced the wooded hills, game of various kinds came forth. The Moon god was, understandably, unappreciative of the manner in which the repast was served, and so violent was his anger that he killed the unfortunate Uke-mochi. However, even in death her body continued its work, for cows and horses emerged from her head, silkworms from her eyebrows, millet grew from her forehead and a rice plant sprang from her stomach. The earliest record tells the story as pertaining to Susano but a slightly later one, the *Nihongi*, makes the Moon god the murderer of Uke-mochi.

Fire Fade and Fire Flash

Physical and climatic phenomena, such as tides and hurricanes, also play a large part in Japanese mythology. Earthquakes, too, are an integral and hazardous part of life in Japan. There were two mythical princes about whom a well known story is told. Their names vary from version to version, and so to avoid confusion, the English names – Fire Fade and Fire Flash – are used here. This tale appears in different forms in the most ancient annals of all. Fire Fade was the younger of the two brothers, and an excellent hunter. Fire Flash was a fine fisherman. They had a competition in order to see if each could excel at the other's sport. Fire Fade not only caught nothing, but lost Fire Flash's fish hook. The elder brother ordered Fire Fade to find the hook. This seemingly impossible task was accomplished in a series of adventures. The Old Man of the Sea advised Fire Fade to sail out to sea in a little boat. This he did and met and fell in love with the Sea King's daughter. In due time they married and found the missing fish hook in the throat of a *tai* or sea bream. Homesickness for Japan (a recurrent mythological theme and still a national characteristic), coupled with the duty of returning the fish hook to Fire Flash, made Fire Fade return to land. His wife, pregnant at the time, gave him the Tide Ebbing Jewel and the Tide Flowing Jewel. These Jewels of the Sea reappear in myths at intervals, being used for various purposes.

The Hira Hurricane

The hurricane around Lake Biwa which often happens in August is called the Hira Hurricane, for it blows from the Hira mountain range. A legend concerning it tells of a young girl who lived on the lakeside and became infatuated with the lighthouse keeper on the other side of the lake. She used to visit him, crossing the water at night guided by the light he kept flashing across the lake. All went well for a time. But her indifference to the dangers of drowning as well as her wanton behaviour suddenly made the lighthouse keeper wonder if perhaps she were an evil enchantress and not just an attractive, brave young woman ready to visit her lover nightly in spite of a perilous voyage. So one night, in order to test his theory,

he put out the light. She got lost on the darkened lake and finally, in fear and rage at the lighthouse keeper for failing to help her reach him, flung herself from her boat. As she drowned she cursed him and his lighthouse. A hurricane blew up at once and did not subside until both the lighthouse and its keeper were no more.

The cherry and the plum

The Japanese love flowers and the indigenous plants of Japan have their myths. Sir Francis Piggott wrote in his *The Garden of Japan*: 'One day Kinto Fujiwara, Great Advisor of State, disputed with the Minister of Uji which was the fairest of spring and autumn flowers. Said the Minister: "The Cherry is surely best among the flowers of spring, the Chrysanthemum among those of autumn." Then Kinto

Right: a clay figure in the Archaeological Collection of Tohuku University in Sendai. It is an object of an ancient domestic cult, but the meaning of the symbols with which it is decorated have not yet been understood.

Bottom left: a wayside Shinto shrine dedicated to the Stone Deity.

Bottom right: Jizo Bosatsu (the Indian Kshitigarbha), Buddhist patron of travellers, pregnant women and children. His effigies are generally of stone and are in the open by the roadside. He is usually shown as a shaven priest. This is a wooden statue in the Saidai-ji Temple in Nara.

Far right: eighteenth century mask. Masks worn by warriors were made of iron and lacquered inside, but those used in Noh plays or dances are made of either plain or lacquered wood. This mask was used in a dance called Gigaku.

said, "How can the Cherry-blossom be the best? You have forgotten the Plum." Their dispute came at length to be confined to the superiority of the Cherry and Plum, and of other flowers little notice was taken. At length Kinto, not wishing to offend the Minister, did not argue so vehemently as before, but said, "Well, have it so: the Cherry may be the prettier of the two; but when once you have seen the red Plum-blossom in the snow at the dawn of a spring morning, you will no longer forget its beauty." This truly was a gentle saying.'

In such a setting, mythological stories about flowers and plants abound. One concerns two grasses, Patrinia and Miscanthus. They often grow near each other, and a story gives the reason for this. A girl, abandoned by her lover, drowned herself. After her body had been

recovered and she had been buried, Patrinia grew from her grave.
Later, in remorse for having driven his mistress to suicide, the man
too drowned himself – in the same river. He was buried beside her,
and from his grave grew Miscanthus.

A small leafed ivy, growing in rocky places, is called *Teika-kazura*.
Teika was a thirteenth century poet who loved a poetess, who also
happened to be a princess. After her death she was buried near a
Buddhist monastery in Saga. In his grief Teika clung to the tomb and
his desolation is perpetuated in the ivy which grows all over it.

Ninigi and the Blossom Princess

Although short life was not always the pattern, there was a time
when the princes of the imperial house were not blessed with old age.
Perhaps this gave rise to the myth that when Amaterasu's grandson,
Ninigi, was sent to Japan with the three items of the imperial
regalia, he fell in love with Ko-no-hana, the Princess who makes
the Flowers of the Trees to Blossom. Her father, Oho-yama, the
Great Mountain Possessor, had an elder daughter, Iha-naga,
Princess Long-as-the-Rocks. Ninigi was given the choice of either
daughter. He remained faithful to the Blossom Princess and
married her. The elder sister, who had wanted to marry the 'Beloved
Grandson' herself, was deeply hurt by the marriage and stated
that had Ninigi married her, their offspring would have lived long – as
long as do the rocks. But now her nephews would bloom and fade
and fall as the blossoms in the spring. In spite of this dire prophecy,
the children of Ninigi and his chosen bride included Fire Flash and
Fire Fade, the latter becoming the grandfather of the first emperor
of Japan, Jimmu Tenno, through his marriage to the daughter of
the Sea King.

After the Sea King's daughter had followed Fire Fade back to
earth and he had returned the fish hook to his elder brother, she
asked him to build her a shelter in which she could give birth to the
expected child. She went into this hut as her labour began and
commanded him not to watch the delivery. Fire Fade did look and
to his horror saw that she had taken on the form of a dragon for her
confinement. He fled from the place of her labour, but on his return
found a mortal boy child in the small building: his wife had
returned to her Sea King father for good, having been seen on land
in her dragon shape. She sent her sister from the sea to look after
the baby and when he reached manhood he married this aunt.
Their child was the first emperor.

Whatever the general life span of the princes of the imperial
family may have been, a grove of cherry trees surrounds the shrine
to the consort of Ninigi, and her father and sister are venerated as
Father Mountain and the Rock Princess.

The crest of the imperial army was a single cherry blossom,
symbolising the glorious if short life of one dedicated to duty.
Bamboo has long been a lucky symbol, representing tenacity and
courage. The bamboo will bend in the wind but not break. It is a
plant which grows profusely in the country and is admired for its
grace as well as for its symbolic meaning. It is used both at
festivals for ornamentation and in varying forms as a crest. Flowers
play a far more important part in the heraldry of Japan than in
other countries. It is the flora rather than the fauna which
predominates in the crests of the old families.

Their gardens show how aware of the beauty of their
countryside are the Japanese. Mountains, deep valleys, terraced
fields, waterfalls, streams and rock formations all find their place in
these often small but accurately proportioned gardens. They are
landscapes in miniature. The plant life and the land in which it
grows are as peculiarly Japanese as the myths surrounding them.

Left: Kishijoten is the goddess of Luck and the sister of Bishamon. She holds the sacred gem in her left hand. The statue is in Joruri-ji Temple, Kyoto.

Raiden, the Thunder god, caught by Uzume, the Mirth goddess, in her bath. The god is usually depicted, as here, as a demon. Victoria and Albert Museum.

Above: netsuke were originally made from carved ivory, bone or wood and used as a stopper or toggle for a box or container. Later they became art forms and this one depicts Uzume, the Shinto Mirth goddess. It was she who was largely responsible for luring Amaterasu from her retirement in the cave. University of Pennsylvania Museum.

Right: Dainichi Nyorai is one of the Buddhist Triratna or Trinity. He is generally shown, as here, holding his left index finger, wearing a crown and seated in meditation.

A HISTORICAL SURVEY

The Toshogu Shrine is among the Shiba Temples in Tokyo. The first Tokugawa Shogun, Ieyasu, is worshipped under the posthumous name of Toshogu, and the Tokugawa crest can be seen all along the eaves of this, the Karamon (or Chinese) Gate of the shrine.

It is not easy to differentiate between the ending of the mythological period and the beginning of the historical period in Japanese history. There are many myths set in historical times: people known to have lived have been turned into legendary heroes, and as the stories have been retold, so have their adventures and deeds grown in number and their heroism been magnified.

The area known as Yamoto in Honshu was certainly the seat of power from earliest times. It was here that the first Emperor of Japan, Jimmu Tenno, ascended the throne in the year 660 B.C., though this date is a legendary one. The story, and mythology in its strictest meaning, goes back further still, into the Age of the Gods.

The *Kojiki* and the *Nihongi*

The earliest extant Japanese book, the *Kojiki* (*Records of Ancient Matters*), was completed in A.D. 712 to be followed in A.D. 720 by the

25

Nihongi (Chronicles of Japan). These are the two main sources of all Japanese mythology and it is from them that the tales concerning the pre- or semi-historic era in the first and other chapters of this book are culled.

It is believed that two earlier sets of records were compiled, but that they did not survive. The Emperor Temmu, who came to the throne in A.D. 673 caused all that was known of their contents to be committed to memory. Hiyeda no Are, who is thought to be a woman, though this has never been conclusively proved, was charged with this task, but her patron died before the *Kojiki*, as the work is now known, was written down. A decade after its completion, having been in Hiyeda no Are's memory for twenty-five years, the *Nihongi* was written. They both appeared in the reign of the Empress Gensho (715-723), but it was the Empress Gemmio (708-715) who commanded that the *Kojiki* was to be recorded at her court from the spoken memories of Hiyeda no Are. In other words, the compilations of legends and beliefs of the Yamato people were made in the eighth century for the purpose of confirming the celestial origins of the court and of the population. The *Kojiki* was kept by the Shinto priesthood in manuscript form until it was printed for the first time in 1664. The *Nihongi* is written in Chinese characters, but the earlier *Kojiki*, while written in the same manner, has peculiarities of purely Japanese syntax and it is this work that established the Shinto orthodoxy.

Oh-kuni-nushi

To reach the mythical period before the semi-historical founding of the empire, it is necessary to return to the Izumo peninsula. The Storm god Susano's activities were chiefly confined to Izumo. His son-in-law was a young god, Oh-kuni-nushi, 'the Great Land Master'. Oh-kuni-nushi secured Susano's daughter in marriage by abducting her. He tied Susano's hair to the beams of his house and then the pair eloped, taking with them Susano's sword, his bow and arrows and also his *koto*, or harp. But Susano was woken by the strings of the koto playing of their own accord as the couple fled, and he followed the sound. When he caught up with the pair, he was evidently impressed by their cunning for not only did he permit the marriage, but he allowed them to keep the treasures they had stolen and, most important of all, gave to Oh-kuni-nushi the right to rule the province.

Suku-na-biko, the dwarf god

Oh-kuni-nushi was greatly helped in his new authority by a dwarf god called Suku-na-biko, 'Small Renown Man.' They first met when he arrived on the Izumo coast on a little raft, wearing moth wings and tiny feathers. The dwarf was the child of the Divine-Producing-Goddess and he was qualified in the medical skills. He and Oh-kuni-nushi became inseparable and together they cured disease in the area and also cultivated plants and crops. The Small Renown Man ended his days by climbing up a millet plant when the crop was ripe. His weight, coupled with that of the ears of grain, caused the plant to bend and then fling him up to heaven. It is said that this endearing little god still appears and leads people to hot springs, an action characteristic of him because he was known for his kindly disposition as well as for his medical knowledge.

Although the state was founded in Izumo, Amaterasu wanted her grandson Ninigi to rule the whole archipelago that had been generated by Izanagi and Izanami. Through a series of intermediaries, including her own son, she made attempts to gain her object. But agreement was not reached until the children of Oh-kuni-nushi and Ninigi himself arranged that Ninigi should rule in Izumo.

There was a proviso that the powers of the visible world should be his and that things 'hidden' should remain the preserve of Susano's descendants. The Small Renown Man's medical knowledge as well as the powers of exorcism and the occult did not come under Ninigi's control. It is worth noting that in the *Nihongi* Susano had the domain of the sea, a whole subterranean world, though this is not stressed in the *Kojiki*.

One of the highest Japanese orders is that of the Sacred Treasure. Ninigi was the first to be invested with it for Amaterasu gave him the regalia of royalty: the Sword, the Mirror and the Jewels. He and his retainers arrived in Kyushu from the Celestial Plains on the Pacific coast, a region called Himukai. In translation, this means, appropriately, 'facing the sun.' They migrated eastwards

Left: wooden statue of Bishamon. Bishamon is one of the seven Gods of Luck and is of Buddhist origin. He is usually shown holding a spear in his right hand and a small temple or pagoda in his left. These are lost in this statue. The creature on which Bishamon stands portrays the forces of evil. Museum für Völkerkunde, Vienna.

Right: a typical Japanese rendering of the Amida Buddha in the Jururi-ji Temple, Kyoto. He became very popular during the tenth century. The faithful hoped to attain Nirvana through his intervention.

Below: the Taira hero, Kiyomori, prays that the sunset be delayed, so that his retainers should not be prevented from finishing the restoration of the temples at Miyajima, a self-imposed task which meant much to the warrior. Print by Kuniyoshi. Victoria and Albert Museum.

along the Inland Sea towards the central region of Honshu known as Yamato, which was not finally reached until two generations later by Jimmu Tenno, who landed on the main island near the present city of Osaka. The descendants of Amaterasu and Ninigi were once defeated by the local inhabitants as they made their way eastwards when they fought facing the sun. Thereafter they always fought, successfully, with the Sun goddess' rays behind them. After Jimmu Tenno's arrival as the first Emperor of Japan, Yamato continued to be the seat of the Imperial court until the end of the seventh century. The court then moved to the present city of Nara, also in Honshu but further north. There it remained until 784. Kyoto became the capital in 794.

It was during the Nara period that the *Kojiki* and the *Nihongi*

Above: the battle of Dannoura. Antoku, the child-emperor, his mother, grandmother, and attendants with Taira-no-Tomomori at the final moment of defeat. Shortly afterwards the mother jumped into the sea with the child in her arms, to be followed by the grandmother. Antoku thus never became the captive of the Minamoto clan. Print by Kuniyoshi. Victoria and Albert Museum.

Top right: Tomomori, a Taira hero, followed the young emperor Antoku to death by drowning rather than live to see the defeat of his cause at the Battle of Dannoura. He is shown with one of his retainers and his mistress under the sea. A ship's anchor is coiled round his neck. Print by Kuniyoshi. Victoria and Albert Museum.

Bottom right: handle of a kozuka, or small dagger, worn at the side of the sword scabbard. The carved relief represents Yoshitsune, his mistress, and Benkei fleeing from Yoshitsune's brother, Yoritomo, after the Battle of Dannoura in 1185. The ghosts of their fallen enemies pursue them. Museum für Völkerkunde, Vienna.

were written down. It was a period of seven reigns and was, on the whole, a creative and constructive era. But centuries before it was established, the court was harried by the Ainu and there was insurrection in Kyushu. The Emperor Chuai (192-200) died from an arrow wound in the Kyushu campaign, though in the *Kojiki* it is recorded that he died while playing upon a musical instrument instead of invading Korea, the territory which the gods had promised him if he would undertake the expedition.

Yamamoto Date

Chuai was the son of Yamamoto Date, one of the eighty children of Emperor Keiko. Yamamoto never became Emperor himself, but he was a mighty fighter and patriot. He lived in the second century and many stories are told about him. He was sent to subdue rebellious tribes in the west in order to avenge atrocities committed by them on some of his numerous brothers. He disguised himself as a young woman and in this way was admitted into the house of one of the tribal chieftains. This chieftain gave a feast in honour of the 'young woman' and became drunk with his own *sake*, whereupon Yamamoto Date stabbed him to death.

Yamamoto felt it his duty to kill another outlaw. He pretended to be ignorant of the man's crimes and became an acquaintance of his to the extent of going swimming with him occasionally. When Yamamoto Date was assured the outlaw had no suspicions he took a wooden sword with him on one of these excursions in addition to his own lethal weapon. While the outlaw was in the water Yamamoto Date swam ashore and, without being seen, took the outlaw's sword from its scabbard, replacing it with the wooden one. In those days one did not go about unarmed. When the swimmer joined him, a friendly duel was suggested and as the victim of the trick struggled to pull the sword made of wood from the scabbard, his opponent decapitated him with his own sword. His father, the Emperor Keiko, was highly delighted to hear of this performance.

On another occasion Yamamoto was sent east to subdue the Ainu tribes. On the way he paused to pray at the shrine where the sword Susano had found in the dragon's tail (now part of the imperial regalia) was kept, and he took the sword with him. The

Ainus pretended to surrender and invited him to hunt with them on an open plain. But they surrounded him and set fire to the undergrowth. He hacked down the bushes with the sword and so escaped. There are other more magical versions of this story. Another incident occurred on the same expedition to the east. His ship was overtaken by a fearsome tempest and his consort, knowing that he had angered the sea gods and that they would not cease to torment him and his party without a human sacrifice, threw herself overboard into what is now Tokyo Bay. The ship was thus able to take Yamamoto Date and his party safely to their destination, for the storm ceased with the suicide.

After further escapades Yamamoto Date returned to his family, and heard of a rebellious evil spirit. Again he went off on an expedition, but became sick of a fever caused by this spirit. He was forced home, where he died. A white bird rose up from his burial mound and the

Right: an image of Bakira, one of the Twelve Heavenly Generals, in the Shin-Yakushi-ji Temple, Nara. The Heavenly Generals are faithful followers of Buddha. Each commands an army of seven thousand acolytes, and defends the eighty-four thousand pores of the skin against disease-carrying demons.

Mitsukuni defies a skeleton spectre invoked by Takiyaske. Print by Kuniyoshi. Victoria and Albert Museum.

same phenomenon occurred at two subsequent reburials. The reinterment of the father of the Emperor Chuai was recorded later and is an example of how the ancient heroes cling in the imagination and their stories become extended.

Conquest of Korea

The year A.D. 200 is not only the traditional date of Chuai's death, but also that of the invasion of Korea by his widow, the Empress Jingo. The exact date of the conquest is uncertain, but it is an integral part of Japanese mythology that the Empress carried her unborn son for three years. This long period between his conception and his birth allowed his mother to complete the subjugation of Korea and return to Japan. In due course the infant

became the Emperor Ojin, who was later deified as Hachiman, the god of War. He became a patron deity of the Minamoto clan who played an important part in Japanese history eight hundred years later.

It is recorded that the kings of the then Three Kingdoms of Korea promised Empress Jingo to 'pay homage and send tribute until the sun no longer rises in the East, but comes from the West; until the courses of the rivers turn backwards and the river pebbles ascend and become stars in Heaven'. Whatever the historians may make of Emperor Ojin's mother's conquest in the third century, her success was believed to be due largely to her having the Tide Ebbing and the Tide Flowing Jewels with her. These mythical Jewels of the Sea, the origin of which has already been described, enabled her to control the tides and thus the manoeuvres of her fleet of ships and the army of fishes which accompanied her. Disappointingly,

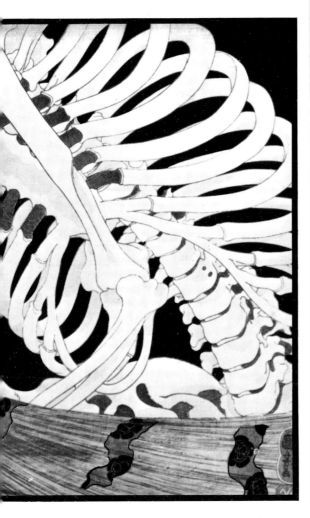

perhaps, there appears to be no connection between jingoism and the warrior empress who gave birth to the god of War.

Certainly the close connection between Japan and Korea is a long established mythological and historical fact. In A.D. 285 one of the three Korean kings introduced Chinese characters into Japan. He did this when his tribute took the form of 'Confucian Analects' and 'One Thousand Selected Chinese Characters'. The written language had arrived – and in its basic form had come to stay.

The arrival of Buddhism

This is not the place to go into the minute details of Japanese history and their interrelation with the history of China and Korea, but three centuries after the Korean tribute which gave Japan a written language Buddhism also came; again from Korea and again in the form of a tribute.

An example of a red lacquer-lined samurai wrought iron battle mask. Such masks were intended to frighten the enemy as well as give facial protection to the wearer. By Myochin Munetomo, 1590. Seattle Art Museum.

Right: seven-inch-high figure of Monju-Bosatsu painted on silk in gold and mounted in a brocade folder. Monju is variously described as the Buddhist deity of Education, Enlightenment and Wisdom. The sword in his hand represents the cutting down of obstacles to Enlightenment. Eighteenth century. Seattle Art Museum.

A Historical Survey

One of the Korean kings was in need of military aid from Japan and his tribute this time took the hitherto unique form of an image of Buddha made of gold and copper, together with a selection of Buddhist scriptures. The *Nihongi* gives the date of this gift (of no less importance in Japan than the arrival of St. Augustine in England) as A.D. 552.

The reigning Emperor received the new doctrines gladly, but there was opposition at court. The details of the emotional and martial conflicts of this period are obscure, but apart from man-made strife, disease also struck. The anti-Buddhists felt that the plague, if plague it was, came from the influence of the new religion and the golden image was thrown into the nearest river and the temple which housed it destroyed. The ravages of illness were temporarily abated, but a sudden flash of lightning from heaven (it was from a clear sky that the lightning came) not only demolished the imperial palace but killed those responsible for the desecration of the temple. Quickly the image was retrieved. But the events were repeated and the Emperor himself became a fatal victim of the recurring epidemic. For a second time, the image was recovered and a new temple erected around it.

Shotoku Daishi

The years 593 and 621 are those given for the real acceptance of Buddhism in Japan. They were the years of the regency of Shotoku Daishi. This was his posthumous name (*daishi* means saint or abbot), for his name during his lifetime was Mumayado. This in translation means stable door. It was given him because his mother, the empress consort, gave birth prematurely when inspecting the imperial stables. He was a law giver and a social reformer as well as being a devout Buddhist, and it is thought that the art of Japanese flower arrangement began during his regency when he insisted on having flowers put in front of his image of Buddha in his private shrine. The great Japanese scholar, the late Basil Hall Chamberlain, called him the 'Constantine of Japanese Buddhism.' The introduction of the calendar is also often attributed to Shotoku Daishi.

It was about this period that Japan received her name. Before it had been a loosely defined territory in and around the Inland Sea, Izumo and Yamato; and it took the name of the latter province. But as the control of the court increased, so did interest in Buddhism, and with both came the flow of learning from the Asian mainland. The term *Jih-pen* in Chinese means 'source of the sun' and the Chinese gave this name to the land to their east. The words Nippon and Japan were easily derived from the original Chinese Jih-pen. Dai Nippon (Great Japan) does not have the same meaning as in Great Britain, where the 'Great' was used to differentiate it from Brittany. Dai Nippon is a literal expression of the feeling the Japanese have for their country.

The Fujiwara period

One of the most famous temples built by Shotoku Daishi was at Nara and it was there that the first capital was built. This Nara Period lasted from 710 until 784. The next period lasted longer, from 784 until 1192. It was the Fujiwara Period. The capital was moved to the present Kyoto ten years after the Fujiwara clan gained power. They were predominant in every way. The era was given their name and they married into the imperial family.

Among Ninigi's attendants when he first arrived in Kyushu was one called Ama-tsu-Koyane. He married and had children and in due time the family became hereditary holders of the title of

A Historical Survey

High Priests of the Empire. In the seventh century one of them took the name of Fujiwara, becoming at the same time the first Minister of State. The civil and religious hold became absolute. The early religious office and influence was, of course, Shinto and not Buddhist. Fujiwara means 'Wisteria field' and the family crest, extant to this day, is yet another example of the use of flowers in Japanese heraldry.

For three centuries the Fujiwaras held sway not only at court, but throughout the land. It has been described as an era of peace and completion. The visual arts and literature were patronised and the *katagana* and *hiragana* scripts were invented during the Fujiwara Period. Both scripts are types of phonetic characters, used to expand the existing system of Chinese writing.

But the long years of court life took their toll and the Fujiwaras began showing signs of decadence. Because they held all the civil appointments the warriors came from other families. These different clans held the borders safe and, as time went on, became not only scornful of the civilian Fujiwaras and their retainers but increasingly skilled in the art of war. Of the great fighting families and clans there were two of outstanding importance: the Tairas and the Minamotos.

The feud of the Tairas and Minamotos

The politics of this troubled era are of no particular concern as far as mythology goes. But the decline of the Fujiwaras and the struggles for power between the Taira and Minamoto clans are. These struggles have been the sources of many myths, ballads, legends and even the themes of plays.

The wars between the two factions lasted thirty years and have often been compared with the Wars of the Roses. The Taira flag was red and the Minamoto white. The dates are 1156 to 1185 and the conflict is sometimes called the Gempei War – Gempei being a combination of the names, in characters, of the two opposing sides. But though we need not consider the detailed politics one thing must be borne in mind: regardless of the person who held the position of Emperor, the loyalty to the monarchy as such was absolute on both sides. There were disputes as to the rightful claimant of the imperial regalia, but throughout these struggles – and throughout the long history of Japan – republicanism was not an issue.

Much of the information about this time comes from an epic narrative, the *Heike Monogatari*. The Minamotos and the Tairas are referred to there and elsewhere as the Genji and the Heike. To avoid confusion the Genji will be referred to by their other name of Minamoto, and the Heike as the Taira clan.

Yoshi-iye

Yoshi-iye was a very early Minamoto hero. He attained his manhood ceremoniously at a sanctuary dedicated to Hachiman, the god of War, and he and the now deified Emperor Ojin became patrons of the Minamoto clan in particular, and all warriors in general. White doves are associated with Hachiman (as they are with Yamamoto Date) and their appearance was always a good omen for the Minamotos in the eleventh century battles. Yoshi-iye, like Yamamoto Date before him, led expeditions against Ainu tribes. On one of these expeditions his soldiers suffered greatly from heat and thirst. Yoshi-iye prayed to Hachiman and then pierced a rock with a powerful shot from his bow, and water gushed forth in a fountain which was never to dry up. Such miracles are told of the very different hero and saint Kobo Daishi, some of whose achievements will appear in other chapters.

A Historical Survey

Kiyomori

The most famous Taira warrior was Kiyomori – head of the clan from 1118 to 1181. He was the hero of the *Heike Monogatari* and died four years before the Battle of Dannoura in April, 1185. There are many tales about him: he was a lustful man and the mistress of his Minamoto rival, Yoshitomo, was forced to submit to him in order to save the life of her young child, Yoshitsune. Against his better judgment at a later date, Kiyomori spared the lives of Yoshitsune and his two brothers, one of whom was Yoritomo. It was Yoritomo who finally defeated the Tairas at the naval Battle of Dannoura. Kiyomori, at the height of his power, married his daughter to the Emperor and their child became the infant Emperor who died in that decisive contest.

Benten, a goddess of the sea, will appear again. But she provides a tale about Kiyomori. As a young man, he saw a small craft with a scarlet sail glowing in the sea off the island of Miyajima in the Inland Sea. There were three fairy-like women on board who revealed themselves to be Benten and her two sisters. Benten promised Kiyomori much glory if he would enlarge her temple at Miyajima. He did this, from ambition rather than piety one gathers, and her prophecy was certainly fulfilled. The scarlet flag of the Tairas derives from Kiyomori's maritime meeting with Benten.

Tametomo and Yoshitsune

Tametomo was the uncle of Yoshitsune, both of the Minamoto family. They have become legendary heroes, though Yoshitsune is the greater of the two. Tametomo fled the capital when he was only fourteen during the time when the Fujiwaras and the military men were endeavouring to overthrow each other. He was a warrior and a leader, and skilled in the use of the bow. He fought with his father in 1157 and after his father's death he was exiled. His last great feat was to sink a Taira ship with a single arrow, after which he committed suicide, thus dying a hero's death. Further heroic deeds are attributed to him and it is said that he went to the Loochoo Islands and founded a royal dynasty there. Stories such as this are so popular that it is commonly believed that he was the first King of the Loochoos.

Yoshitsune's exploits are many and his name and that of his retainer, Benkei, echo down the years. A number of their adventures have been dramatised in the Noh plays. They were both twelfth century adventurers and they were victorious over the Tairas. The legends about Yoshitsune, as about his uncle, extend beyond the time of his known death. The story goes that after his demise, caused by his elder brother's jealousy, instead of dying he went to Yezo (the present Hokkaido) and even that he became Genghis Khan himself.

Battle of Dannoura

The last battle between the Tairas and the Minamotos was the battle of Dannoura in the Straits of Shimonoseki. Yoshitsune was one of its heroes and his brother, Yoritomo, the victor. But the Tairas showed extreme gallantry, many of them choosing to commit suicide rather than submit to defeat. The mother of the baby Emperor, Antoku, Kiyomori's daughter was among these, leaping from a Taira ship with her child in her arms, entrusting herself to the mercies of the gods and goddesses of the sea. At the same time, the sacred sword was lost. Malcolm Kennedy in *A Short History of Japan*, states that the rest of the imperial regalia was later recovered.

Small crabs, known as Heike (Taira) crabs, are indigenous to this part of the Inland Sea. They have indentations in their shells which look like a scowling human face. These crabs are believed to hold the spirits of the drowned Tairas.

Aizen-Myoo. This Buddhist deity represents sexual love changed into desire for Enlightenment. The lion in his hair and the furious face with three eyes are supposed to portray the suppression of passionate lusts. Statue from Nara.

Left: Bishamon, sometimes known as the Guardian King of the North, has been taken by Japan as one of her Seven Gods of Luck. The pagoda and spear with which Bishamon is generally represented have been lost. Painted and lacquered wooden image of the fourteenth century. Seattle Art Museum.

A man confronted with an apparition of the Fox goddess. Print by Kuniyoshi. Victoria and Albert Museum.

Yoritomo, Yoshitsune's elder brother, then set up his own headquarters at Kamakura. He became the first shogun, and the real power in Japan was to remain at Kamakura, or later during the Ashikaga shogunate at Kyoto, until the capital was moved to Yedo in 1590. The court followed from Kyoto in 1868, at which time the name was changed to Tokyo. The court, however, remained in Kyoto for many years. The emperors were supreme in that they reigned there: the shoguns ruled in Yedo from the end of the sixteenth century.

Family strength is again exemplified by the rise of the Hojos. Hojo Tokimasa and his son, Yoshitoki, were the father-in-law and brother-in-law respectively of Yoritomo. They seized power shortly after his death and their family ruled as shoguns (although they did not actually take the title) until 1333.

It was in the year 1281 that Kubla Khan sent an invasion armada to Japan. The story is not unlike that of the Spanish Armada. The few Mongols who succeeded in landing were quickly defeated; their fleet was destroyed by a great wind believed to be of divine origin.

By this time the social pattern had become, under the imperial court and shogunate, a system of *daimyos* or governors, feudal lords, and *samurai,* their retainers. The rest of the population had no share in either political or military affairs.

Insurrection followed by periods of peace characterised the Middle Ages. During the Ashikaga shogunate (1338-1573) civil disturbances were interspersed with periods of luxury and culture. The Noh plays were largely written in this era and the arts of flower arrangement and the tea ceremony developed. The famous Gold and Silver Pavilions (the Kinkakuji and Ginkakuji) were built in Kyoto as residences for the shoguns.

Toyotomi Hideyoshi

Another period of clan struggle for power and territorial gain lasted between 1573 and 1603. Oda Nobunaga (1534-1582) defeated the last of the Ashikaga shoguns (who had Minamoto forebears) and minor chieftains in the Kyoto area. He was assassinated by one of his own generals with the result that Toyotomi Hideyoshi became all powerful. This great warrior and patriot has many times been called the Napoleon of Japan. He was of lowly birth and said to have been sandal bearer in his youth to Nobunaga. He is also unique in being the only Japanese before the twentieth century to rise to great power from humble beginnings. He became a samurai and he killed the disloyal assassin of Nobunaga eleven days after his master's murder. Many were Hideyoshi's subsequent exploits. He not only suppressed uprisings in the southern islands but subdued Sendai in northern Honshu.

His emperor made him commander-in-chief and regent, and in less than a decade following Nobunaga's death, Japan became not only unified but the possessor of a new tax arrangement which led to the end of the old feudal system.

In his lifetime Hideyoshi persecuted both Buddhists and Christians with the object of obtaining complete political power. The first Christian martyrs in Japan, twenty Japanese Christians and six Franciscan priests, were crucified in Kyushu in 1597.

The conquest of China was planned, but Korea refused to participate and Hideyoshi led an expedition to that country. It proved to be unsuccessful. He died before the withdrawal of Japanese troops, commending his five-year-old son, Hideyori, to the care of his generals, one of whom was Ieyasu Tokugawa. While the mightiest of the fighter Hideyoshi's exploits at the end of his life were the most unproductive, there is no doubt that he laid the foundation of modern Japan.

Centre: statue of Jizo-Bosatsu. The staff with six rings is typical of this much depicted deity: the jingling of the rings warns of his approach in case he should inadvertently step on some living creature. Painted and lacquered wood, fifteenth or sixteenth century. Seattle Art Museum.

Far right: two Buddhist recluses, Kanzan and Jittoku. They are often depicted in a cave with Bukan Zenshi and his tiger, and on these occasions they are known as the Four Sleepers. In this picture they are surrounded with temple and kitchen utensils and their robes are decorated with coins. Thus they are shown as wealth deities. Victoria and Albert Museum.

Right: wooden statue of Aizen-Myoo, 1281. Musée Guimet.

There is an unhappy case of repetition in history here. Nobunaga had two sons and planned to found a dynastic line. His loyal follower, Hideyoshi, laid these plans aside. It was likewise with Hideyoshi's small son. Hideyori was entrusted to the care of Ieyasu, but for all his loyalty he too behaved as Hideyoshi had done to the sons of his chief.

The death of Hideyoshi was followed by the Tokugawa shogunate. Ieyasu Tokugawa, who traced his descent to Yoritomo Minamoto, victor of the Battle of Dannoura and the first shogun, seized power. After quelling rebels he became shogun in 1603 and his family retained the power of that office in Yedo until 1867. A flower again is used as the family crest, consisting of three hollyhock leaves, their pointed ends facing inwards, forming a circle.

The isolation of Japan

Christianity was originally brought to Japan in 1549 by St. Francis Xavier, after the West had made contact first by Marco Polo and later, in 1542, by Portuguese sailor-explorers. The third Tokugawa shogun exterminated Christianity in 1624 – Japan does not lack her Christian martyrs – and closed the country to all foreign intercourse (only a few Dutch and Chinese traders were allowed into Nagasaki). So began two hundred years of isolation. In Japan

39

itself it was a period of self-determination and consolidation. The Kabuki theatre was started in the seventeenth century and all the arts, from flower arrangement to the making of screens and brocade, flourished.

The samurai class and their ethics had been firmly established for several centuries by 1702. That was the year in which two feuding daimyos gave future dramatists and story tellers the Forty-Seven Ronin. *Ronin* means 'wave man': someone tossed about in a wave-like fashion. These forty-seven were in fact samurai, and after the daimyo they served had been insulted and then committed suicide with honour, they scattered and were forced to become ronin. They were actual people and the location of their graves is known. Their deeds to avenge their master's death have passed into legend.

Foreign contacts

The year 1853 brought this long seclusion from the outer world to an end in the form of Commodore Perry with his American naval squadron. The Western powers had been unable to negotiate trading facilities, anchorage in Japanese ports, or security for those shipwrecked off Japan until this American commodore with his 'Black Ships' arrived at Uraga. The next year there was a Treaty of Commerce with the United States of America, to be followed by treaties with other powers and the opening of Yokohama to foreign trade.

In 1860 the first Japanese diplomatic envoys went abroad. That same year a notice appeared near the Tokugawa shrines in Nikko. It was dated July 1860 and read as follows: 'To the Tengu and Other Demons. "Whereas our shogun intends to visit the Nikko Mausolea next April, now therefore ye Tengu and Other Demons inhabiting these mountains must remove elsewhere until the shogun's visit is concluded." (Signed) Mizuno, Lord of Dewa.'

The mythical tengu creatures will appear in other chapters, but belief in them was an official historical fact only just over a century ago.

In 1867 the fifteenth Tokugawa shogun resigned power. The year after, supreme authority was restored to the Emperor. This marked the final end of feudalism. The Emperor Meiji came to the throne a year before the Restoration, at the age of eighteen. He died in 1912, and in that period Japan, not without internal difficulties, became a modern nation and was on its way to becoming a great power. It had a new constitution, drawn up in 1889 by the Prime Minister, Prince Ito, with foreign advisers. It had defeated both China and Russia. Korea had become part of its empire and as a result of the Anglo-Japanese Alliance of 1902, Japan joined the Allies in the First World War.

Some of the names of the legendary figures and heroes of Japanese history have appeared already; some will appear again.

THE BELIEFS AND DEITIES OF JAPAN

Left: Fujin, the god of the Winds, is generally depicted, as here, with a bag containing his winds across his shoulders. This statue is in the Ninna-ji Temple in Kyoto.

Right: the Rokuharamitsu-ji Temple in Kyoto was founded by the priest Kuya-Shonin in 963. He carved an eleven-faced Kwannon in the temple in an attempt to stop an epidemic which was afflicting the city at the time. He is generally depicted, as in this statue at the temple, with a staff in his left hand, a hammer in his right and a gong suspended from his waist. This originates from the story that once, when on a pilgrimage, he struck the gong every time he had prayed ten times. He is shown in this statue invoking the Buddha, his hammer and gong at the ready.

Buddhism has a very important influence on Japanese mythology. There are many stories of Buddhist monks laying ghosts, of men turning to the seclusion of a Buddhist temple in remorse. The badger, an animal which repeatedly appears in Japanese folk lore, is often depicted in the guise of a Buddhist monk. But Shinto not Buddhism is the indigenous religion. It is from Shinto that the authentic Japanese mythology comes, from the *Kojiki* and the *Nihongi*. When Emperor Temmu (673-686) arranged for the 'Records of Ancient Matters' – the *Kojiki* – to be memorised by Hiyeda no Are, he was in fact commissioning a 'history of the Emperors and of matters of high antiquity.' He did this because he wished to avoid future corruptions of the 'exact truth' and to ensure that the generations to come would fully understand not only the story of the creation of Japan but the divine ancestry of the monarch. The annals in both the *Kojiki* and the *Nihongi* are thus, as well as the main sources of mythological tales, the records of 'The Way of the Gods', the short meaning of Shinto. The *Kojiki* in particular settled the orthodoxy of the cult.

Structure of Shinto

It is a cult in which the life of the spirit after death is accepted, but which has no moral teaching. Rewards and punishments after the cessation of earthly life have no part in old Shinto. They came after the introduction of Buddhism. Another important difference between the two is that Shinto has no iconography of its own. Shinto consists of both nature and ancestor worship, but it is the veneration of the Sun goddess, Amaterasu, and her relations and descendants, which is the cornerstone. The attendants who accompanied 'the Beloved Grandson', Ninigi, to Kyushu from the Celestial Plains became Shinto priests.

The pantheon of gods and goddesses is great. Eight million is the figure given, but others have been added as the ancient heroes have been deified. By the time Izanagi and Izanami were created there were eight deities. The pair created Japan and in its mythology the figure eight recurs continually. The dragon with the sword in its tail had eight heads, and is just one instance of this. An example of an addition to the galaxy of gods is Hachiman, the god of War and the son of the Empress Jingo, an Emperor himself in his lifetime, with the name of Ojin.

Everything, be it an animal, a mountain or a tree, has a *kami*: the story of the creation accounts for this belief. Kami has been translated as a soul, a spirit and a deity. Another possible translation of the word is 'beings placed higher'. It is a vitality peculiar to humans and also to things not mortal, among which are included plants and lakes. Nature, in other words, is inhabited by kami. The kami of a mountain may be and often is a deity: it can also be the protector of those who live on or near it.

Since early Shinto did not preach moral codes, 'follow the genuine impulses of your heart' was the core of the teaching, coupled with obedience to the Emperor. Loyalty and filial piety came later, with Confucianism and Buddhism in the sixth century. Purification did play an important part, however. Izanagi purified himself after returning from Yomi, the Land of Gloom, in pursuit of Izanami. His purification is described in the *Nihongi* as being by ablution. The first channel he selected had strong tides and so he had to choose a less hazardous place. Exorcism and abstention are the two other methods of purification and both are performed by priests. The priesthood is not bound by rules of celibacy and one can assume that many of those who became monks in some of the legends related here and elsewhere were Buddhists.

Shinto and Buddhism

That there were opponents to the introduction of Buddhism, itself a thousand years old when it came to Japan from India, via China and Korea, and that support was given it by the Regent Shotoku Daishi (593-621) is well known. Indeed the word Shinto was first used after Buddhism came to the country to differentiate the old beliefs from the new. Until then, it had not been necessary to give 'the Way of the Gods' a name.

There was an uneasy religious situation for some two hundred years, but largely, though not entirely, due to Kobo Daishi (774-834) a compromise was reached through the doctrine of Ryobu or double-aspect Shinto. This is also sometimes descriptively called 'Shinto with two faces' in English. Another great Buddhist priest of the same period was Dengyo Daishi (767-822) who introduced the Tendai Buddhist sect to the country. Kobo Daishi was responsible

for the Shingon sect. Shinto, like Buddhism, has its sects.
Japanese chivalry, *bushido*, was greatly influenced by
Zen Buddhism. The Kamakura shoguns (1185-1392) stressed the
importance of mental and bodily discipline. In the chapter on heroes
the will-power and self-control of bushido – the samurai spirit – will
be apparent. Ryobu Shinto, like Zen Buddhism, has an
influence on myth and legend. The two priests, Kobo Daishi and
Dengyo Daishi, gave to Buddhism a nationalistic trait, hitherto
absent, and regarded the array of Shinto gods and goddesses as
manifestations of the Buddhist pantheon. It was not a big step
after this acceptance to identify Amaterasu with Dainichi Nyorai,
'the primordial and eternal Buddha'. There was and still is much
overlapping of the deities.

For nearly a thousand years it was the norm for Buddhist priests
to take services in Shinto temples, but the exceptions were in Izumo
and at Ise, where Amaterasu's shrine still exists. Architecturally
the scene changed too: the simplicity of the Shinto shrine was
overlaid by the ornamentation of the Buddhist. However, with
the 1868 Restoration, came a revival of the early Shinto precepts –
the divine ancestry of the Emperor being paramount – and so
'pure' Shinto was revived and became once more the national

*Left: a standing figure of Juichimen, the
eleven-headed Kwannon, Buddhist god of Mercy.
It is made of several pieces of wood and has the
remains of smoke-blackened gilding on it.
Kwannon is shown in various forms of which the
eleven-headed version is one. Probably seventeenth
century. Museum für Völkerkunde, Vienna.*

*Right: Amida Buddha standing between two
seated figures dressed as bodhisattvas. They have
filigree crowns on their heads. Gilded wood.
Museum für Völkerkunde, Vienna.*

religion, but not the only one. Buddhist priests left the temples; pagodas, belfries and other appurtenances not associated with Shinto were removed, and undoubtedly much of historic and artistic worth was destroyed. As far as buildings for worship were concerned, it was a situation akin to England under Henry VIII.

Buddhism was in no way suppressed. The two religions merely separated, but the influence of each on the other in the various sects remains to this day, and Ryobu Shinto is still extant.

The torii
For the uninitiated, the simplest way of distinguishing a Shinto temple from a Buddhist one is by the simplicity of the former and because it has a *torii*. This gateless entrance is frequently depicted

Right: Zocho of the South, one of the Shi Tenno, the Four Guardians who keep the world from the attacks of demons. Kofuku-ji Temple, Nara.

Far right: Tadanobu, reputed to be one of Yoshitsune's retainers, belongs to history, as a gallant soldier at the Battle of Yashima during the wars between the Taira and Minamoto clans, and to legend. Part of the legend is that he was a fox-man and another part is that when Yoshitsune had to take flight he left his mistress in the care of Tadanobu. At this time he gave the woman a drum made of fox skin and the story goes that a fox, the child of the vixen whose skin had been used to make the drum, took on the form of Tadanobu in order to reclaim the relic of its mother. Tadanobu is here shown in the guise of a fox. Painting by Baikoku. Victoria and Albert Museum.

with its two upright posts and a single or double cross bar. The purpose of it is a much discussed issue. The word is not unlike that meaning bird, *tori*, and doubtless this gave rise to the idea that the torii were designed to provide resting places for birds and also to give warning to the gods of the approach of daybreak. But the more likely reason for the torii is that it marked the place where that which was sacred was enclosed. Certainly the torii is an intrinsic feature of places which are holy to pure Shinto and to Ryobu Shinto.

The sakaki tree
The *sakaki* tree is mentioned in the *Nihongi* index four times (W.G. Aston's translation): it is a tree sacred to Shinto and is variously described as Eurya ochnacea and Cleyera japonica. Certainly before the Second World War branches of the tree were laid on the altar in the Yasukuni Shrine in Tokyo. Yasukuni is the national

Shinto shrine dedicated to those who died in defence of their country: their spirits are enshrined there and it has been described as the Valhalla of Japan. The first mention of the sakaki tree in the *Nihongi* concerns Amaterasu. Among the desecrations performed by Susano when humiliating his sister, 'he secretly voided excrement under her august seat' and she 'was sickened'. She then retired to the cave. Jewels were made and also the mirror, and the Mountain god was charged with making eighty (the figure eight again) combs out of the five-hundred-branched 'true sakaki tree', while the Moor god made an equal number of combs from a form of grass. Later in the same story a mirror of 'eight hands' together with jewels were hung on the branches of 'a true sakaki tree' and then it was that Amaterasu peeped out of the cave and light returned to the world.

Susano is given the domain of the sea in the *Nihongi*. The accounts of his activities range from the obscene to the heroic. One legend about him shows an aspect totally different from either of these characteristics. He received kindness from a poor man and in return told him how to prevent his home from ever being ravaged by the Plague god. The method was simple: to hang a platted straw rope across the entrance of his house. It must have been efficacious, for the custom of preventing the spread of epidemics by hanging such ropes along roads persists. The straw rope is also used as a symbol of conjugal union. In Futami in the province of Shima, two rocks, 'Wife and Husband Rocks', lying near the shore are tied together with such a rope.

Tengu and oni

Tengu are associated with Shinto: *oni* with Buddhism. These mythical creatures are described in the following chapter. Shinto

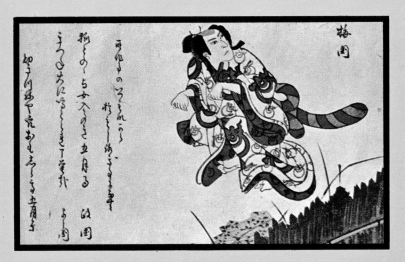

shrines have, not always but often, pines and cryptomerias growing in the vicinity and these trees were generally believed to be the habitations of the tengu. Of the many tales concerning the oni, or devils, there is one which particularly stresses the Buddhist connection. A travelling monk met an oni – horrible as usual in appearance but, as was not usual at all, in floods of tears. Curious and compassionate, the monk asked the reason for its sorrow. The oni had been a human being in its previous existence and because he had at that time been consumed with thoughts of revenge towards an enemy had been turned into a devil on his death. In that state he had had every opportunity to wreak vengeance on his enemy and also on the man's descendants, for oni have a far longer life span than mortals. The weeping oni had just killed the last of the family line and his tears were not of regret for the vengeance wrought, but self-pity because he would have to live the rest of his oni life with

Below: painting of Bishamon, holding his characteristic spear and temple, in the Kofukuji Temple at Nara. The temple was originally built there in 710 and destroyed by fire during civil strife in 1717. The painting dates from the thirteenth or fourteenth century.

The Beliefs and Deities of Japan

a desire for revenge on the family, which could not be fulfilled, now that the family was extinct.

Shrines and curses

Shrines are sometimes associated with curses. There are tales of unhappy or wrongly used people having shrines erected to their memory, in order to enclose their spirits and prevent the curse from spreading. In one such story a brother and sister fled from their enemies, possibly during the long period of civil unrest in the Middle Ages. They hid in a cave and were fed there by a woodman. This protector made his mother promise she would not betray the pair. She did not do so directly but when questioned by the pursuers of the couple, she glanced towards the place where they were hiding. After an intensive search, they were found and beheaded. The resulting curse was that the woman's neck became bent and she could never hold it straight again and her descendants suffered from eye ailments. One shrine was built for the brother, another for the sister, and while one does not know if the other family's eye trouble continued, an epidemic in the area which followed the unhappy incident did not recur.

Mirrors

The mirror into which Amaterasu gazed was housed at her shrine at Ise, or so the story goes. Certainly mirrors have a place in sacred edifices, as Amaterasu's does in the insignia of the Order of the Sacred Treasure. There are two proverbs which sum up the significance of the mirror in mythology. One is: 'When the mirror is dim the soul is unclean' and the other runs: 'As the sword is the soul of a samurai, so is the mirror the soul of a woman'. According to the *Kojiki*, Izanagi gave his children a highly polished silver disc and told them to kneel before it each morning and evening and examine themselves. He said they were to subdue their passions and evil thoughts so that the disc could reflect only a pure spirit. The mirror is thus part of ancient Japanese tradition.

There is a famous story known as the Matsuyama Mirror, which does not have a strictly pious connotation. It deals with mother-love rather than romantic love. Matsuyama, which means Pine Tree Mountain, is a place and also a surname. The mirror of Matsuyama is generally accepted to refer to the place rather than to the name of the family in whose possession it was.

A man gave his wife a metal mirror which he had bought on a visit to Kyoto and which was engraved on the back with the symbols of long life and married union, the pine tree and a pair of cranes. Cranes are believed to have, like mandarin ducks, only one partner in life. The wife had never seen her reflection before and while the gift delighted her it embarrassed her also to see her beauty.

This couple had one child, a daughter, as pleasing to look at as her mother and very like her. When the girl was in her early teens her mother became ill and for months she nursed her as the wasting disease destroyed her parent's looks. Just before the woman died she gave her daughter the mirror, carefully wrapped, saying that it was her most precious possession and would comfort the child in her sorrow.

The girl had not previously seen the mirror, and when she opened the package after her mother's death she thought her own reflection was her mother, young and beautiful again. She used to murmur to the reflection and, seeing the animation on the face, believed she was communicating with the dead woman, and thus found consolation in her grief.

The story varies from version to version. In one the father married again and the step-mother thought the girl was muttering incantations

*Right: head of a wooden statue of Miroku-bosatsu.
Miroku is supposed to be Buddha's successor
due to appear five thousand years after Buddhas's
arrival in Nirvana. Miroku is not among the
popular Japanese deities although it is said that
Kobo Daishi, founder of the Shingon sect, preached
of his importance, and is reputed to be waiting
in his tomb for Miroku, in a state of ecstasy.
This statue is in the Muro-ji Temple in Nara.*

*Below: Hachiman, the Shinto god of War.
Wood cut, mounted as a kakemono, or hanging
scroll. Museum für Völkerkunde, Vienna.*

into the mirror. After much misunderstanding the truth was
discovered and the three lived happily together. In another, the
father worried about the child's repeated withdrawals to her room
to whisper to the mirror; again, when the explanation was given,
the story ends with a serenity understood to have been bestowed by
the devotion of the mother and the influence of her mirror.

The bell of Mugen

In one of his works, *Kwaidan*, which was published in 1904,
Lafcadio Hearn dates the legend of the bell of Mugen to 'eight
centuries ago'. It was and is not unusual for bronze mirrors to be
given to temples for making bells or images. Hearn writes of seeing
a collection of such mirrors which had been contributed so that

a bronze statue of Amida might be cast. In Mugenyama at the time
of which Hearn wrote, a similar collection of mirrors was made for
a temple bell. One woman gave her mirror which she had inherited
from her mother, who had in turn inherited it from her mother. Apart
from being an heirloom, the mirror was important to the woman
because of the design of lucky emblems engraved on its back: the pine,
the bamboo and the plum. She regretted having given it away, and
she feared for the truth of the proverb of the mirror being the soul of
a woman. When the time came for the great bell to be cast, the
mirror given by the woman would not melt. As the villagers knew
who had donated it, her shame was great. Her heart was revealed to
all as being hard, as hard as the metal of her gift. She had given her
heirloom with reluctance and, further, had regretted the giving. No
wonder the metal remained solid when the other mirrors, given
in a different spirit, melted under heat.

Eventually her spite, growing like a cancer within her, became so overpowering that she killed herself in anger, leaving a note to the effect that after her death, the mirror she had given would melt and that great wealth would come to whoever managed to break the bell incorporating the metal. This note was in fact a curse and the woman's spirit was a vengeful one, dying as she did in a state of bitter anger.

After the bell was cast, it was beaten constantly by those who tried to break it and obtain the promised worldly wealth. The resulting incessant bell-clanging for this impious reason and, one would imagine, the disturbing noise, finally prompted the priests to roll the large temple bell down the hill below and push it into the swamp at the bottom, where it lies still, leaving only the legend behind.

The ghost of O-Sono

Another story shows a spirit anguished in a totally different way. O-Sono was the daughter of a wealthy provincial merchant. Her father had sent her, well chaperoned, to the capital which was then Kyoto to learn the gracious skills such as the tea ceremony and flower arrangement. After her return to her father's house, she was married to the son of a family friend, also in business. The couple had at least one child, a boy, but the marriage was short-lived, for after four years O-Sono died. Not long after her death her son said he had seen his mother in her bedroom. Other members of the family also saw the ghost of the dead woman, always looking at the *tansu*, a chest of drawers containing her clothes. Her mother-in-law suggested her clothes and belongings be taken to the local temple, for if O-Sono's spirit was enjoying them still it was better it should do so in sacred precincts. This was done, but the ghost still appeared. Then the temple priest – a Zen Buddhist according to Hearn – came to the house, again at the instigation of O-Sono's mother-in-law. He stayed in the bedroom alone and the ghost duly appeared and gazed at the tansu. He opened each drawer in turn, but all were empty. Still the ghost of O-Sono looked sadly at the piece of furniture. Then the priest took the lining paper from the drawers, and in the last and bottom drawer he found a letter addressed to O-Sono under her maiden name. She nodded and bowed her thanks when he told her he would take it to the temple and there burn it and that no one should read it but himself. It was a love letter O-Sono had received during the period she was finishing her education in Kyoto. Its contents were never revealed and no one, neither the writer nor any of her family, was caused any distress. The ghost of O-Sono never appeared again.

The celibate monk

Another story concerning a Buddhist is similar to the one about the lighthouse and its keeper, for it is about the Hira Hurricane on Lake Biwa. A celibate monk was the object of a sudden and deep passion of a young woman. He was young himself and the temptation to yield to her emotion was great. In order to avoid having to see her, he told her he was a hermit living at the foot of Mt Hira and that if she could cross the lake a specified number of times at night in a washtub, he would give way to her desire. The monk clearly thought the feat to be impossible and he could not believe she would even attempt it. However, the young woman not only attempted it, but succeeded in making the dangerous journey in the totally inadequate vessel the requisite number of times, until the last night. Then a violent storm blew up and she was drowned, her passion proved but unrealised and the monk's celibacy maintained. The hurricane rages still at the time of her death, so great were her longings.

A netsuke of Hotei, one of the Seven Gods of Luck. He is a cheerful and contented deity and is often shown in the company of a child or children. As usual, he is depicted with a large naked stomach and a kindly expression. British Museum.

The Beliefs and Deities of Japan

En No Shokaku

In the seventh century, there lived a Buddhist saint called En No Shokaku. He climbed various mountains, including the eight-peaked Haku, in order to bring them and other hitherto inaccessible places to the notice of Buddha. He was finally condemned as a magician for his miracles. By the use of mystic signs he caused the swords of his executioners to snap and then he suddenly received the gift of flight, for he flew away and was never seen again.

Kobo Daishi

Although Dengyo Daishi played an important part in paving the way for Ryobu Shinto, there are few legends about him. It is known he made a journey to China and stayed there for a long time and

Right: Kwannon of a Thousand Hands. In this representation Kwannon is encircled by many arms as well as having multiple heads. Wooden figure from the second half of the tenth century.

Far right: a typical country shrine in the outskirts of Nikko.

brought back with him the tenets of the Tendai sect. Of his contemporary, Kobo Daishi, the legends are legion. One concerns a grove of chestnut trees, which bear fruit earlier than is usual. It is said that a travelling priest once promised little children who were not able to climb trees then growing there at chestnut time, that the following year they would be able to gather nuts. From that time on, the trees in the area have borne fruit before growing to their full height, and the priest of the tale is thought to be Kobo Daishi.

There is a statue of Jizo, the Buddhist guardian of the souls of dead children, though he cares for others too, near Lake Hakone, carved from the local grey basaltic lava. The image is believed to be over a thousand years old and it is alleged that Kobo Daishi carved it in a single night.

He also had encounters with creatures from the other world. It is said that he was forced to endure visitations from evil spirits during his training for the priesthood. Later, dragons and sea monsters disturbed him while he was in meditation. He was able to drive them back to their watery habitations by reciting mystic words and also by spitting at them. It was no ordinary saliva which helped him rid himself of their presence: light from the Evening Star had magically come into his mouth and it was rays from this which he ejected in the direction of the creatures. He built a temple to commemorate the cessation of these visits from the beings from the sea, but even so was haunted by other malevolent spirits. Finally he enclosed the new temple with sacred signs and the building was troubled no further by tormentors from the spirit world.

He was known as a sculptor and traveller, and, of course, as a preacher and miracle worker too. Apparently he painted also, and

the calligraphy known as the *Hiragana* is attributed to him. He was born at Shikoku with his hands folded in prayer. A fox tried to deceive him on his home island when he was preaching there and that is why he is said to have driven all foxes from Shikoku. It is still said in places in Japan where there are no mosquitoes that Kobo Daishi banished them in perpetual gratitude for hospitality he received there.

Kobo Daishi travelled continually, often disguised as a wandering beggar, and hospitality must have played an important part in his life. On numerous occasions he is reputed to have rewarded the generous and punished the greedy. It is said that he repaid an old woman who gave him water, although she had little, by striking his staff on the ground and creating a fountain near her home. This is only one example of his miracles. On another of his journeys a villager refused to give him potatoes to eat, with the excuse that they would be too hard to offer a guest. Kobo Daishi replied that if that were so then it should be so always. The man's crop of potatoes from then on was inedible as they would not soften when boiled.

According to another legend, he once washed his clothes in a river. As happened so often, he was in the garb of a travelling beggar and the villagers did not recognise him as the preacher he was. They taunted him, presumably for polluting their river. He left that village and went to another nearby river and there washed his clothes and received no local criticism. The first river still dries up in the summer and the other flows all the year round. It is also believed that no deaths by drowning have occurred in the latter river. All this is attributed to Kobo Daishi's miraculous powers.

Kobo Daishi lived until the age of sixty, but it was asserted after

his death that he had in fact gone into the tomb to wait for the coming of Miroku, the Buddhist Messiah – and is still waiting there at the monastery he founded at Koya-san, near Nara.

Several stories relate to his creation of wells or fountains. There is a shrine of extreme antiquity near the Kita-ura Lagoon called Kashima. The name means Deer Island, but the place is not an island any more. The temple itself is said to have been founded in the Age of the Gods: certainly it is very old. Near it there stands a stump of worn stone which is supposed to be a pillar, the foundation of which is at the centre of the world. This stone is known as the Pivot Stone, and is believed to have a restraining influence on the great fish whose wild thrashings cause earthquakes. Kobo Daishi was praying to the god of the Kashima shrine in Tokyo (then Yedo) when he put his staff into the earth. Water gushed forth from the spot, and the miracle worker afterwards commemorated the occasion by planting a willow tree by the well that had been built to contain the flow of water. The well has since been called the Willow Well.

Mito Komon

Mito Komon, who lived many years after Kobo Daishi, from 1622 to 1700, was a daimyo and kinsman of the Tokugawa shogun family. He was much influenced by the school of thought which favoured the return to 'pure' Shinto and one of his descendants had much to do with the destruction of many of the Buddhist temple treasures, for which he was imprisoned by the shogun in 1840. But of Mito Komon himself, it is told that he tried to find the bottom of the Pivot Stone, an object belonging to the old form of Shinto in which he believed so devoutly, for it was his earnest wish to restore to Japan the

Far left: a porcelain Kwannon, deity of Mercy.

Left: the Buddhist deity Fudo. He is the Waterfall god and, as in this case, is often shown seated on a precipice. He has two attendants, one of whom, Seitaka Doji, is shown here. Fudo carries in his right hand the sword of justice and in his left the rope with which he binds enemies of the Buddhist faith.

Right: Yakushi-nyorai is a Buddha associated with healing and is venerated as such chiefly by the Tendai, Shingon and Zen sects. This statue of him is in the Yakushi-ji Temple in Nara, founded in 680.

beliefs as they had existed before the advent of Buddhism and the subsequent Ryobu Shinto.

Nichiren

Nichiren lived in the thirteenth century and originally belonged to Kobo Daishi's Shingon sect of Buddhists before founding his own, which bears his name. Indeed, at the age of twelve he became an acolyte and joined the priesthood when still a boy. But his sanctity appears to have come even earlier, for his mother became pregnant as the result of dreaming of the sun shining on a lotus flower. Nichiren means Lotus of the Sun. The year of his birth was 1222.

One of Nichiren's miracles is similar to En No Shokaku's of an earlier age, for when condemned to death by the Hojo Regent Tokimune, the executioner's sword could not decapitate him. Tokimune himself was warned in a dream of the dire consequences of killing this holy man and did not pursue the death sentence, although Nichiren was banished to the Island of Sado for three years. At the end of that period, in 1274, he was allowed to go to Kamakura, the seat of government. But soon afterwards he went to live in a hut in the mountainous area of Minobu. One of his disciples gave him and all members of the sect his land in that district in perpetuity, and as his flock grew Nichiren built a shrine which later became the monastery of Minobu. After his death his ashes were taken to Minobu.

Hachiman Taro, named after the god of War, but also known as Minamoto-no-Yoshiie belonged to the eleventh century. One of the earliest Minamoto leaders, he subdued the north of the main island Honshu, and was responsible for the area coming under the imperial domain. One of the stories of his military prowess or acumen is that by noticing the sudden startled flight of wild geese he discovered an ambush and accordingly routed his opponents. His life was a fighting one, but in his old age he became a Buddhist monk, as did others of both the Minamoto and Taira clans.

Another man raised to the company of gods lived a century earlier than Hachiman's namesake. His name was Tenjin and he was not a warlike character but a scholar. However, he had enemies and through a series of misrepresentations had to end his life in banishment. During his last exile he is reputed to have used a bull as a mount and temples dedicated to him often have images of bulls in their grounds. He became the god of Calligraphy for his learning, but he was a man who appreciated plant life as well as being a scholar and a man of great physical courage. His crest was a formalised plum blossom: the plum is believed to have been his favourite tree. A plum tree from his garden is said to have taken to the air and floated from Kyoto across the sea to join him in Kyushu where he was exiled until his death.

Images

Images of many kinds are prominent in Japanese mythology, particularly those that symbolise various Buddhist beliefs. There are stories of images taking the form of their followers in order to save them from death or disaster. The statue of Kwannon, the goddess of Mercy, in a village is said to have saved the life of a young local woman. This woman used to worship the Kwannon with regularity each evening. Her husband was jealous of the nightly pilgrimage, for he did not appreciate that she left their home to go to the shrine and he began, as time went on, to imagine a very different assignation. One evening he hid by the road near their house and as his wife returned he slashed her savagely with his sword. On his return home he was much startled to find her waiting for him. She told him she had felt very cold suddenly on her way home, but in no other way made reference to the attack upon her. The husband must have spent an uneasy night, wondering who had been his victim, and the following morning he went to the place where he had waited the previous evening. He found splashes of blood there which led from the roadside to the shrine, and on the shoulder of the Kwannon he saw a deep cut, in the very place where he had believed he had slashed his wife. It is said this ill-tempered man confessed his deed and one is curious to know how his wife reacted to his behaviour towards her. Her constant supplications to the goddess of Mercy suggest that he cannot ever have been a gentle husband.

One of the images of Jizo, the patron deity of travellers, pregnant women and children, bears a scar on its face, allegedly from a wound received when it took the form of a boy who was about to be attacked. In the other world a haglike creature is believed to rob children of their clothes and cause them to heap stones endlessly on the banks of the Buddhist Styx. Images of Jizo often have pebbles piled round them, in an attempt to assuage the labours of these unfortunate children.

Nichiren's escape from decapitation took place near Kamakura, and in that city, among a great number of temples and mausoleums– including that of Yoritomo, the first shogun who made the place his capital – are the temple of Hachiman, the temple of Kwannon and the huge bronze Buddha known as the Daibutsu. It is told that when Yoshitsune fled to the north to escape from his elder half-brother Yoritomo, his mistress was taken to Kamakura for questioning as to her lover's whereabouts and was forced to dance at the Hachiman temple for the entertainment of Yoritomo.

The image of the goddess of Mercy in the Kamakura shrine is

Left: kakemono by a Shinto priest. The figures represent two ancient smithy deities with carpenter's tools. Nowadays they are venerated chiefly by carpenters. Ink and colour wash on paper. Eighteenth century. Museum für Völkerkunde, Vienna.

Right: painting of Jizo. Jizo's images and portraits abound in Japan. He bears in his left hand the jewel that grants wishes and in his right the shakujo (staff) which mendicant priests carry. Koya San Museum.

thought to have been installed in 736 and is carved from half of a camphor tree. The image is just over thirty feet tall and the legend is that the other half of the tree was used for the statue of Kwannon in Nara. It is also said that when the Kamakura statue was made, it was thrown into the sea with a prayer that the world would be redeemed of sin at the place where it floated ashore. This place is on one of the Kamakura beaches where Yoritomo is reputed to have practiced archery centuries later. It was near the Temple of Kwannon that Yoshisada in 1333 threw his sword into the sea, an incident described in a later chapter, and it would seem that the temple was already there at that time.

The bronze Daibutsu in the Todai-ji Temple in Nara. It is reputed to be the largest bronze image in the world, being 53½ feet tall, but it lacks the beauty of the Daibutsu in Kamakura. The Nara Daibutsu was finished in 749. Twice the hall in which it stands has been destroyed by fire and it is thought that only some of the lotus leaves and the trunk of the body are original. It is also believed that when it was first made the statue was gilded.

The Daibutsu

Of the holy places in Kamakura the one most frequently depicted is the Daibutsu: photographs of it appear on travel advertisements to this day. It is ninety-seven feet in circumference at its base and is about fifty feet in height. It is made of bronze and was cast in 1252: Yoshisada must surely have seen it. Originally the statue was housed in a wooden building, but this was destroyed in a violent storm in 1369. The Buddha was undamaged, as it was in 1494, when a tidal wave swept away the rebuilt structure surrounding it. Since then the statue has sat serenely exposed to the elements and survived the violence of both sea and earthquake. Yoritomo, it is alleged, thought of having a huge image of Buddha in Kamakura, by then his capital, when he took part in a ceremony of consecration of an image of Buddha in Nara. He died before the artist, Ono Goroemon, finished the work at Kamakura. The original wooden pillars (and there were said to be sixty-three of them) supporting the edifice around the statue have, of course, gone, but some of their stone bases remain. The Daibutsu has miraculously survived the years, just as the image of Buddha which was brought from Korea in 552 survived being thrown into the river on two occasions.

The storms of 1369 and 1494 were historical events, but there is a legendary story concerning the preservation of the Daibutsu. Soon after the Daibutsu was in position in Kamakura, news of its vastness reached a whale living in the sea in the north. It was disbelieving: nothing could be larger than itself. However, stories reached the whale, from fishermen and fishes, of the fame of the statue and the numerous pilgrims who visited it. The whale's disbelief turned to curiosity and jealousy, and a shark who was friendly towards the whale offered to swim south and get measurements of the image. This was difficult for the shark, but by seeking the assistance of a rat about to disembark from a fishing boat, he was able to give the whale the exact size of the base of the Daibutsu. The rat scampered around the image, counting its footsteps as it went. It had to take five thousand paces to complete the circle. The whale, on receiving this information, put on magic boots in order to see the statue itself: doubtless its intentions were malicious. With these magical aids, having reached the beach, it was able to walk to the building in which the Buddha was then housed, but owing to its great size it could not squeeze inside and see the statue for itself. However, a priest came out and, with less surprise than normally would be expected, asked the whale its business. The whale demanded to know the height of the statue. Then the Daibutsu came down from the pedestal and was as surprised as the whale to meet, face to face, a being of similar size and girth. The statue agreed that its measurements should be taken by the priest, who used his rosary for the purpose. The Daibutsu was found to be two inches shorter and thinner than the whale. The whale's pride was satisfied, the image had acted peaceably and the priest must have been satisfied, if shattered, by the whole experience. The whale returned to its home in the north, and the Daibutsu returned to its sitting posture of benign calm, where it has remained to this day. It is reputed that images of Buddha whine if they are stolen: apart from the conversation with the whale the Daibutsu has always been silent.

F. Hadfield Davis advances the theory that the legend grew out of the fact that the gigantic Buddha is out of keeping with the usual art forms in Japan: metal workers, wood and ivory carvers and lacquer artists are all masters of the miniature. He also speaks in *Myths and Legends of Japan* of two differential measurements, the whale measure for soft goods and the metal foot for hard material, the difference in the two being about two inches.

Hotei, one of the gods of Luck. He is thought to have a good-natured temperament and is always willing to do acts of kindness such as carrying a woman across a stream.
The naked abdomen is the feature which generally characterises Hotei.

Inari, the Rice god

Inari, the god of Rice, is sometimes shown as a bearded man, but there seems to be confusion as to Inari's sex, for the deity is also known as a goddess. The messenger of Inari is the fox and the god or goddess is depicted as a fox, too, on occasion. Inari is regarded as the patron of swordsmiths and, in more recent times, of traders generally.

The god of the Rice Fields comes down from his mountain home in the spring and returns in the autumn, and this may have some connection with the old Shinto belief that mountains possess spirits or gods. The mountain cults have no part in this book, but the very shape of some of the Japanese peaks suggest a phallic symbol, and these symbols do play a part in the rites of such cults. The gods of the Roads, too, are associated with the phallic cult, but there may be no real connection. When Izanagi left the Land of Yomi he was subsequently chased by Eight Thunders – this, before he performed his ablutions – and he threw a staff on the road and in their path, saying they should pursue him no further. Sticks are used in the phallic cults in that the stick is the *shintai* of phallicism as well as of roads. A shintai is an object in which an invisible deity can incorporate itself to contact believers.

The seven gods of Luck

The seven gods of Luck or Good Fortune are naturally very popular among the Japanese. Hotei is a peculiarly Buddhist one. His distinguishing feature is a huge stomach, below which his garments sag. This does not symbolise greed. On the contrary, it is a symbol of contentment and good nature and the protruding abdomen is believed to be symbolic of Hotei's large soul. He has inner resources,

Above: kakemono of Fukurokuju, one of the Gods of Luck. He is recognisable, as always, by his high domed head. Ink on paper. Copy of fifteenth century work. Museum für Völkerkunde, Vienna.

Above top: Daikoku, the god of Wealth and one of the Seven Gods of Luck. The rice bale, protruding stomach and cheerful expression are all typical of portrayals of this deity. Musée Guimet.

Centre: the Seven Gods of Luck together in a boat, with Mt. Fuji in the background. The only goddess among the seven, Benten, is in the centre of the picture. Victoria and Albert Museum.

typical of one who has successfully acquired serenity through Buddhist wisdom.

Jurojin is the god of Longevity. He is always shown in the company of a crane, a tortoise or a stag – each representing contented old age. He has a white beard and generally carries a *shaku*, a sacred staff or baton on to which is fastened a scroll containing the wisdom of the world. Jurojin also enjoys sake, but in moderation. He is never a drunkard.

Fukurokuju (or Fukurokujin) has a very long and narrow head, and the luck he typifies combines longevity and wisdom. His body is exceedingly short and his head is often shown as being longer than his legs. He evidently did not originate in Japan, for in his earthly life he is said to have been a Chinese philosopher and prophet.

Bishamon is sometimes regarded as the god of Wealth, but that is Chinese Buddhism. The Japanese have included him in the group of gods of Luck and he is always shown dressed in full armour, carrying a spear. But he is no Hachiman, for in his other hand he carries, in typical Buddhist fashion, a miniature pagoda. These two objects show that he is intended to combine missionary zeal and the warrior attributes.

Daikoku is the god of Wealth. He is also the guardian of farmers and is a good-natured and cheerful god. He carries a mallet which can grant wishes made by mortals and he sits on a couple of rice bales, with his non-vegetable treasure slung over his back in a sack. Rats are sometimes shown eating rice from the bottom of his bales: Daikoku's good humour and wealth are such that he cares not at all.

Ebisu, another god of Luck, is a hard worker. The example he sets is one of honest labour. He is the patron of tradesmen and fishermen, but only the fishing aspect of his activities is depicted for he carries a fishing rod and also a *tai*, sea bream.

And finally there is Benten, the only goddess among the seven. She has already appeared in the second chapter and will appear again, for the myths surrounding her are many. She is associated with the sea and many of her shrines are either by the sea or on islands. This association is often shown in her pictures and statues, when she is riding or is accompanied by a sea serpent or dragon. She also represents the arts and general feminine deportment. Her favourite musical instrument is thought to be the *biwa*, a string instrument not unlike a mandolin in shape.

The shrine and the carpenter

It is inevitable that the construction of shrines and of temples should give rise to a variety of myths and legends. In feudal times a daimyo wished to build a holy place: it must have been a Shinto shrine rather than a Buddhist temple, for it was a skilled carpenter he needed, rather than an artist or sculptor. But the daimyo was unable to

Another portrayal of Hotei, again identifiable by his naked abdomen. Ink and colour wash on paper. Museum für Völkerkunde, Vienna.

Right: Ebisu and Daikoku, two of the Gods of Luck. The latter is on the left of the picture. As so often he is depicted holding a hammer and cheerfully disregarding the rats nibbling at his store of rice. Ebisu is the patron of hard work and is usually associated with fisherman and the sea, as can be seen in this representation. Kakemono painted in colour wash and ink on silk by Hokurei, 1851. Museum für Völkerkunde, Vienna.

find a local carpenter sufficiently experienced for the task and the shrine remained an idea only. However, a travelling carpenter heard of the daimyo's dilemma and offered his services, saying he would do the whole assignment by himself on the sole condition that he should not be watched while at work. The daimyo accepted this and instructed those in the village not to stare at the newcomer at his task. At the end of the first day's work the daimyo passed by and noticed that the lone carpenter had made a great deal of progress. Every evening it was the same: it was hard to believe the building was the work of only one man. One night, when the village streets were deserted the daimyo went to the site of the shrine and was much astonished to see not the walls of the new building waiting for their creator to return in the morning, or even the carpenter himself, but many men working there. They all looked exactly like the carpenter the daimyo had hired, and they were all working in complete silence.

The daimyo assumed the man had collected his friends to help with the work and did not wish to offend the villagers by flaunting their carpentry skills. Clearly the time had come for the payment to be made: the building was already nearing completion. As the team of silent workers all looked identical, the daimyo asked the one nearest him which was the original carpenter whom he had hired. He was soon identified by a small birthmark on his face. He accepted the money due to him and gave no explanation for his colleagues being there, indeed he was as silent as the rest of them.

When the shrine was finished, which was not long afterwards, the carpenter disappeared from the area and so did his mysterious helpers. Later still, a number of straw dolls were found not far from the shrine and the assumption is that these had come to life at the behest of the stranger, each assuming his physical appearance and craftsmanship and, presumably, his piety.

A netsuke of the Seven Gods of Luck sailing together in a treasure ship. Only four of the pantheon are visible in the photograph. Victoria and Albert Museum.

Tengu

The *tengu* are among the strangest of Japanese mythological creatures and also among the oldest. Some say they are descended from Susano, the brother of Amaterasu. They are minor deities, respected and feared as such, and the old belief in them still persists. They inhabit trees in mountainous areas, generally seem to be associated with pines and cryptomerias, and live in colonies with a principal (or king) tengu in charge, who is served by messenger or 'leaflet' tengu. They are part bird and part man in appearance, winged with long beaks or noses. Sometimes tengu are red in colour and they often wear cloaks and small black hats. They are good swordsmen (as was shown by the skill with the sword which they imparted to Yoshitsune) and are mischievous rather than evil in character. Sometimes they are depicted as wearing cloaks of feathers and sometimes of leaves.

Fond of playing tricks themselves, they are unappreciative of the reverse.

A youth, who flouted belief in the supernatural, disguised himself as a tengu and climbed into a tree, where the local villagers saw and venerated him. But he fell to his death and all thought this to be the vengeance of the tengu whom he had flagrantly impersonated. In another tale, a boy teased a tengu by pretending he could see the wonders of the heavens by looking through a hollow piece of bamboo. The tengu, distraught with curiosity, eventually succeeded in getting the boy to part with the stick by exchanging it for his straw cloak of invisibility. The boy played many tricks on his family and friends when wearing this cloak, but the tengu who had been deceived exacted its revenge and the boy fell into an icy river, lost

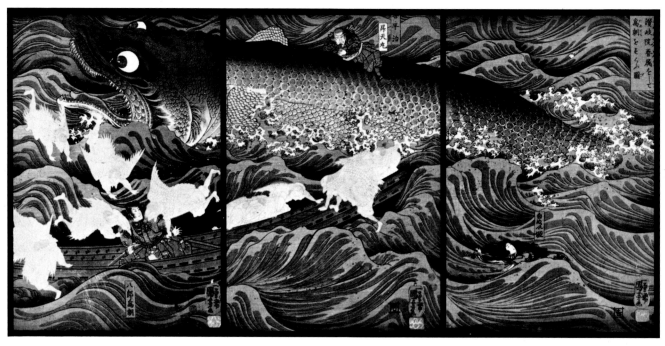

The twelfth-century legendary Minamoto hero Tametomo being attacked by a giant fish and rescued by a flight of tengu. His wife and servant are also shown in the picture. Print by Kuniyoshi. Victoria and Albert Museum.

Right: Shoki wrestling with two oni, or devils. Shoki is of Chinese origin, Chung Kw'ei, the Demon Queller, but he has been incorporated in Japanese art for several centuries. British Museum.

the magic cloak and lived to appreciate the danger of taunting tengu.

Oni

Oni frequently appear in the old legends. They are devils, often of giant size. They can be pink, red, blue or grey in colour. They generally have horns and occasionally three eyes. Three toes and three fingers are other distinguishing features of the oni. They can fly, but seldom seem to use this ability. While occasionally they are comic creatures, they are usually cruel, malicious and lecherous. Intelligence does not appear to be among their attributes. They are believed to have originated in China and to have come to Japan with the Buddhist faith. Often, as on the occasion of Issun Boshi's encounter with a pair of them, they carry a mallet – as does Daikoku, the god of Wealth – and it is not uncommon for them to be depicted carrying an iron spiked rod and wearing a loin cloth of tiger skin. Both Momotaro and Yoshitsune with Benkei rescued young women from being captives of oni. There is another tale which well exemplifies their delight in the human female and their lack of intelligence.

A bride was travelling to the village of her future husband when a cloud descended over the vehicle and transported it and its passenger out of sight. The bride's mother immediately left the procession and began a search for her daughter. After a solitary and unavailing journey, she came across a small temple inhabited only by a priestess, who gave her shelter for the night. The mother learned from this hostess that her daughter was the captive of a group of oni

in a castle on the other side of the river. The bridge was guarded by two dogs, and to reach her missing daughter she would have to cross while the dogs slept.

The following morning the bride's mother found herself alone on an open plain: the temple and the priestess had been supernatural and had vanished completely. However, there was a river, a bridge and two sleeping dogs as the priestess had described. The woman crossed and found her daughter weaving in the mansion on the other side In spite of the apparent dangers of their situation, the daughter cooked her mother a meal, then hid her in a stone chest before her captors' return. But the chief oni had made her his special property and when he got home he knew there was another human in the house, for he had in his garden a magical plant which produced a flower every time a mortal ventured in oni territory. The girl had the inspiration to say she had just discovered she had become pregnant, which must account for the second flower on the plant. The explanation delighted the oni so much he gathered his retainers around him and they feasted until they became drunk. Eventually the oni who claimed the young woman as his own demanded that she put him to bed. He slept in a wooden chest with seven lids, and the girl locked her abductor down into his sleeping place. During the revelries the guard dogs had been killed and so the mother and daughter had no fears about their escape. They went to the building where various vehicles were kept and as they were wondering which to choose, the priestess who had given the mother shelter suddenly appeared and advised them to take a boat and sail away down the river.

The oni in his wooden chest woke up with a thirst induced by his surfeit of sake, broke the seven lids and called for the girl to bring him water. He then wakened his retainers from their drunken sleep and together they all staggered to the river, only to see the two humans sailing away. The group of oni flung themselves down on the river bank and began to quench their thirst. As they drank the river level lowered and the escaping craft was drawn back towards them. Again the priestess appeared and came to the rescue. She urged the mother and daughter to open their kimonos and expose themselves to the oni. As there was evidently no other method of getting away, they did this as did the priestess herself. The spectacle excited the oni: they laughed and guffawed with delight, to the extent of coughing up the water they had drunk. So it was that the river filled again and the little craft floated away to safety.

Before she disappeared for the last time, the priestess told the grateful mother and her daughter that in reality she was a stone statue and in return for her services to them she would like another statue to be placed near her each year. One can understand that it must be lonely to be a statue. Somehow the two women found the priestess in her stone form and caused similar companions to be placed beside her once a year from then on. Whether the daughter ever did marry her human bridegroom is not known.

In another story the villain is a female oni. A young priest in training asked his master for permission to go into the woods to pick nuts, but at first he was not allowed to go for the oni women were known to be in the vicinity. However, eventually the priest gave in to the younger man's repeated requests, saying that he must take with him three lucky charms which would help him should he fall into oni hands. The youth had gathered a few nuts before being captured by an old oni crone and forced to spend the night in her house. The following morning he thought of a means of getting away. He told the oni he had a pain and must relieve himself. She did not want to let him out of her sight and made various suggestions as to where he might perform this function, but he insisted on going

Right: there is a close association between kappa and cucumbers. One of these mythical creatures is shown riding on the vegetable. Painting by Hokuga. Victoria and Albert Museum.

A giant spectral cat and a cadaverous ghost appear in a print by Kuniyoshi. Victoria and Albert Museum.

to the proper place. Finally she tied a cord around him and let him go, keeping a firm hold on the piece of cord. Once he was alone, the young man freed himself and fastened the cord to a beam, at the same time asking one of the lucky charms to answer for him when the oni called.

He climbed out of the window, leaving the charm behind. The oni jerked the cord, but it remained firmly tied to the beam and the charm, lying on the floor where the young man had left it, said in the youth's voice he was not yet ready to come out. However, in due course she realised he had escaped and went in search of him. She, being an oni, was able to travel much faster than her escaped prisoner and soon caught up with him. He flung the second of his charms to the ground, begging it to create a great mound of sand.

The mound appeared immediately and the oni had difficulty in climbing over it, giving the man time to cover a considerable distance. But she caught up with him again, and in despair he threw his last charm over his shoulder, beseeching it to cause a wide, swift river to flow between him and his pursuer. Again his request was granted and the oni woman was washed away in the torrent.

The tale does not end there. At last the young man reached the temple and the priest took pity on him, determined to save him, for they both knew the oni would be relentless in her search for the man who had three times managed to evade her. The priest hid the younger man in a large box which he then hoisted up to the ceiling. The oni duly arrived and demanded her victim.

Denials were in vain, and after a lengthy discussion the priest said he would open the box if she would do exactly as he told her. To this she agreed. He commanded her to grow tall, but when she was nearly able to reach the box he countermanded his order and told her to become short. He left her getting smaller and smaller until she was the size of a bean. Then he quickly picked her up, wrapped her in a piece of dried seaweed and ate her. Only then did he lower the box and let his pupil out, presumably regretting he had ever allowed him to go out in search of nuts. After a while the priest really did have to defecate, unlike the younger man in his first escape. To his considerable discomfort, the priest passed a swarm of flies. The oni had been turned into these and she was never able to resume her old appearance.

Kappa

The kappa is a creature of more intelligence than the oni and is by no means wholly malevolent, in that it can be placated by man and has been known to impart certain skills, notably bone-setting, to humans. Some believe that the kappa is of Ainu origin, others that it is

descended from the monkey messenger of the River god. Kappa resemble monkeys, but have no fur. They sometimes have fish scales or tortoise shell instead of skin. They are approximately the same size as a ten-year-old child, yellow-green in colour and with an indentation on the top of the head, which is their main distinguishing feature. If the water in this hollow is spilled, the kappa immediately lose their powers. They live in rivers, ponds or lakes and are vampires, feeding upon their prey through the anus. Horse and cattle blood satisfies them as well as does human blood. A body with a distended anus found after death by drowning used to be thought to be the victim of a kappa, as indeed would a drowned child or adult whose body was not recovered.

Kappa are also said to be capable of raping women, a character-

istic that they share with the oni. Apart from blood, they have a liking for cucumbers and one way of placating them is to throw cucumbers with the names and ages of the family into the water where kappa live. They will then not entice these people into their clutches. Another feature of the kappa is its capacity for keeping a promise, and there are many stories in which a bargain between man and kappa is struck, to man's advantage. In spite of their many distasteful habits, they are strangely polite, often to their own undoing, for by bowing to an intended victim the water can be spilled from their heads and their strength dispersed. The story of the kappa and the loan of bowls which appears later is an example of a kappa's trustworthiness and courtesy. One of the recurring facts about encounters with kappa is that if a human being is challenged to single combat with one, it is essential to accept, and hope that the kappa will not keep its head erect throughout the encounter.

Far left: Dainichi, one of the Buddhist trinity. He bears a dog's head, the eleventh sign of the zodiac, on his crown. Museum für Völkerkunde, Vienna.

Left: some of the hands of Kwannon of a Thousand Hands in the Toshodai-ji Temple at Nara. This temple was founded in 756 and it is said the preaching hall there at one time was part of the Imperial Palace.

Right: Fudo with his two attendants. The rope in Fudo's left hand is used to bind wrongdoers whom he has frightened with his sword. Eighteenth century. Victoria and Albert Museum.

The human can then extract a promise from it while it is in a weakened state.

There was one kappa which looked deceptively like a child and used to ask those who passed by the pond where it lived to play pull-finger with it. Its victims were then pulled down into the water and never seen again. A man on horseback was able to vanquish this kappa. He locked fingers with the creature but then urged his steed into a gallop. Water was spilled from the kappa's head and it cried out for mercy, promising to teach the man how to set bones in return for its freedom. The man released his hold on his prisoner and later learned all the kappa had to teach him. When he finally let the kappa go, he extracted another promise to the effect that it would make its home elsewhere and not molest human beings again. This promise was also honoured. It is claimed that among the man's descendants there was at least one skilled bone

67

Kintaro, the Golden Boy possessed with supernatural strength, is sometimes portrayed as one of Yorimitsu's four lieutenants. In this capacity Kintaro killed the giant spider, using a tree trunk as a weapon. Even as a child, he could uproot trees with his bare hands. Print by Shunyei. Victoria and Albert Museum.

surgeon. The kappa knowledge passed down the mortal generations.

In another kappa story one of the creatures came out of a river and attacked a tethered cow by putting its hand up its rectum. In its struggles to escape the cow twisted its rope around the kappa's arm and at last the creature returned to the water, leaving its arm, broken off at the shoulder, behind. The farmer who owned the cow found the arm when he came to fetch his animal in the evening and took it home with him.

Later that night the kappa came to the farmhouse, begging for the return of its limb, saying it would be able to fix it onto its body if it were given back within three days. The man did return the arm, but not without first obtaining a pledge that no animal, child or adult in the village would be molested again. The river where this episode happened flows into the sea by a sandy beach and the word of the kappa was honoured to the extent that a supernatural voice used to be heard on the shore on occasions when children were playing there. The voice warned if there was an unwelcome guest on the beach, in the form of another kappa not restrained from attacking humans within its grasp. In this way both the seashore and the river banks in the vicinity became safe from kappa assaults.

The Snow Woman

Female mountain spirits – *Yama-uba* – are sometimes believed to be terrifyingly hideous creatures. But this is not the general rule as will be seen in the case of Kintaro's mother whose story is told later. Another female spirit capable of causing great fear is one which has been written about chiefly by Lafcadio Hearn: *Yuki-onna*, the Snow Woman. She is a ghastly, ghostly white spirit and her custom is to appear in snowstorms and lull men to sleep and subsequent death. She is young and has an extremely beautiful body and a seemingly gentle disposition. Hearn told of two men, one much younger than the other, who took refuge in a mountain hut during a blizzard. During the night Yuki-onna came in and breathed over the older man and then came to the younger. She told him she would spare him if he promised never to mention her visit to anyone.

The old man was dead in the morning and his companion, in his fear, let it be assumed he had frozen to death, the victim of natural elements rather than of a supernatural being. In time he met and married a graceful and gracious young woman named Yuki. This name means snow, but is a usual one and had no sinister connotation for the bridegroom. Yuki proved to be a loving wife and good mother, as well as being a dutiful daughter-in-law. After some years of marriage the husband told Yuki one evening that, sitting as she was with a white light on her face, she reminded him of an episode of his youth. He then spoke of Yuki-onna's visit to the hut and of his companion's death. Yuki's appearance and natural colour changed and she sat revealed as the Snow Woman. In quiet fury she reminded her husband of his promise never to repeat the story and told him that if it had not been for their children she would have killed him instantly. Instead she melted away, never to reappear to her mortal family.

Love between mortals and spirits

The tales of marriages between humans and spirits are varied, ranging from the marriage just described to those with spirits of the vegetable world. In one such story a man greatly admired a willow tree which grew in his village. He prevented it from being cut down to provide timber for a needed bridge, presenting the village with the necessary wood from his own property. Soon after this he met a girl under this willow tree and promptly fell in love with her. She reciprocated his feelings and they married, he well knowing that she

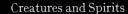

Right: Dainichi-nyorai, a Buddha of Wisdom, who is regarded as a light divinity, and as an incarnation of Buddhist law. Wood, Kamakura period. Museum für Völkerkunde, Vienna.

Far right: another statue of the popular Jizo. The staff with which he is generally shown is missing. Wood. Museum für Völkerkunde, Vienna

Amida Buddha. The position of the hands forming a double triangle is the mudra of meditation. Hollow wood, eighteenth century. Seattle Art Museum.

Creatures and Spirits

had no parents or home. Their marriage was entirely contented until the news came that at the command of the Emperor the willow tree had to be cut down to rebuild a temple. The man's efforts to save it were this time unsuccessful. As it was felled, his wife told him that it housed her spirit. He held her tightly, but neither physical nor spiritual love could keep her with him, and she died as the tree crashed to the ground.

There is another story of love between a mortal and a tree spirit. A pair of lovers met one evening and the man suddenly told the woman that he knew he would die the following morning. He then vanished, leaving her both miserable and mystified. She saw fleetingly the shadow of a pine tree against the *shoji*, the paper sliding door of the room. She was puzzled because she knew pines did not grow in her garden. The following day a pine tree on the outskirts of the village was cut down to replace a bridge which had been swept away in a local flood. Hearing this, the woman remembered her vision of the shadow and went at once to the place and found that, in spite of the efforts of many people, the felled tree remained immovable. She instinctively realised she had loved this tree in its human form: and when she touched the trunk and took hold of one of the ropes attached to it, it shifted easily. Perhaps this was the only way, in death, the tree spirit could prove his identity. His human love for her he had proved before.

Animals transformed into humans

Animals take human form as will be shown again. The fox is well known for this ability, as are the serpent and the badger. In one of the fox stories a husband discovered his wife was in fact a fox by seeing her brush hanging from beneath the quilt when she was in

bed. She had no evil intent though, and indeed helped her husband
with his rice field by arranging for the hitherto unsown field to be
magically planted with plants upside down. Because of this he was
excused from rice tax, although the rice ripened all the same. She also
devotedly nursed their invalid child, whose illness had prevented her
husband from tending his land. For all its strangeness, it was a good
marriage. It may well be that the fox wife was one of the messengers
used by Inari, the god of Rice.

There are many examples of such transformations of creatures into
human form. This type of story is very popular and shows many
variations. A motif frequently appearing is of a serpent taking the
shape of a suitor. In one such story a handsome youth paid attention
to a girl who found him attractive. He was clearly of a higher social
standing than her own, but neither she nor, it appears, any member
of her family could discover where he came from or even his name.
Naturally enough, being flattered by his frequent calls to her parents'
house and becoming emotionally drawn towards him, the girl's
curiosity became unbearable. At the suggestion of her nurse or lady's
maid, she stuck a threaded needle into his outer garment on one of
of his visits to her home. After giving her suitor a start, the girl and
the older woman set out together, following the strand of thread.
It led them deep into the country and eventually disappeared into a
secluded cave. To their alarm they heard groans coming from within.
The nurse lit a lamp, which she had providently brought with her
(one wonders if this courageous and devoted person suspected the
outcome of their search), and went in. A huge serpent was writhing
there, moaning fearfully, for a needle was stuck deep into its throat.
The girl ran away, but the nurse died of fright immediately and
apparently the serpent perished shortly afterwards.

There is another story of a serpent taking human form, but with a different outcome. Two such creatures, again of great size, were found by a hunting party. One was killed but the other escaped. Afterwards much damage was done to the surrounding crops, seemingly by a large marauding animal. Various attempts to find and kill the beast were made, but only the surviving serpent was ever seen. It managed to escape its hunters in spite of being wounded.

At about this time the local doctor was visited by a woman patient, a stranger to him and the area. He dressed a wound which she told him she had got while chopping firewood. When the wound was healed, after several visits to him, she said she could afford no fee, but instead of payment gave him warning of an earthquake which would shortly cause the deaths of many in the vicinity. He accepted this form of remuneration and left the village for a while, thus escaping a devastating earthquake. It appears he shared his pre-knowledge of the disaster with no one, a selfishness out of character with the manner in which he earned his living. Needless to say, this stranger patient was the serpent whose mate had been killed and whose death she avenged first by damage to property and later by far worse damage and death. This story is set in and around Shimbara. Balls of fire are said to be seen at certain times of the year moving across the sea off the coast there. Some believe they are the spirits of those who lost their lives in the earthquake.

Another and totally different transformation legend concerns a cat and is set on the island of Sado. An old couple had a black cat to which they were much attached. They were exceedingly poor and when their hardship seemed to have no solution, the cat, in return for their sacrifices for it down the years, turned into a *geisha*, taking the name of Okesa. She thus made money for the couple though at considerable cost, for apparently she did not relish the life, which involved having sexual intercourse with her customers as well as giving them the more formal entertainment of conversation, singing and dancing, at the last of which she was particularly adept. One of her clients, a boatman, once caught a glimpse of her in her cat form, eating. She made him promise not to reveal her true identity. But when taking a boatload of passengers to Hokkaido, he could not resist the temptation of telling them that the famous dancing geisha of Sado was really the cat belonging to the old couple, and in the circumstances it is hard to blame him. But it is said that a dense cloud appeared in the sky and from it a vast black cat appeared and snatched him from view. The passengers apparently escaped unharmed: they had, after all, only listened to the story. One can still buy dolls doing the Okesa dance. It is a story much told, depicted and danced.

A reincarnation story

Lafcadio Hearn retells a reincarnation story about a girl named O-Tei. She was betrothed to a young man nineteen years of age: she was only fifteen. The couple were genuinely fond of one another, in spite of their engagement having been arranged by their families through go-betweens in the old approved manner. O-Tei became ill with consumption and it became apparent to her as well as to her fiancé that she had not long to live. On the evening before her death she said she would return to him with a stronger body. He vowed to wait for her, but she could not tell him how he would be able to recognise her when she rejoined him. After her death he wrote his promise to marry her if she should ever come back to him, sealed the note and put it by her memorial tablet. Some years went by and in due course he married again, at the instigation of his family, and had one child. His parents died and their deaths were soon followed by those of his wife and child. The comparatively young

A Kirin. This is a mythical Chinese animal quite often met with in Japanese art. It is generally surrounded with flames. Painting by Royen. Victoria and Albert Museum.

Opposite: Amida enthroned in paradise. Musée Guimet.

widower set off on a journey in an attempt to find consolation in his quadruple grief, and while staying in an inn in a village hitherto unknown to him, he was waited upon by a girl remarkably like O-Tei.

Although he had been fond of his wife, he had always been loyal to the memory of his first love, and the old passion was rekindled at the sight of the girl in the inn. He enquired her name and said she reminded him of someone he had known and loved years before. She told him she was called O-Tei and then, in the voice he used to know so well, said she knew of the written promise he had made to marry her should she return to him. This vow had eased her spirit, she said. Then she fainted. Of course they did get married and a joyful marriage it was, but after that initial conversation in her new body O-Tei had no recollection whatever either of her previous existence or of the talk they had together after he had become a widower.

The self-seeking samurai

A traditional ghost story also concerns a marriage, but with a less happy outcome. During the period when Kyoto was the capital of Japan a man, reputedly a samurai, lost his means of livelihood through the financial misfortunes of the daimyo he served. He took employment in another province and although his wife was a good woman he abandoned her, thinking it would be in his best interests to make an entirely new life for himself. As he began to regain his prosperity he took another wife. It was a loveless match and a childless one. His first marriage had been childless, but for different reasons. In due course he became very rich indeed, and realised that throughout the years he had been away from Kyoto he had missed his first wife, indeed, that he really loved her. For the second time this self-seeker left his wife, and returned to the capital. He went to his old home and there found his first wife, looking very little different in spite of the passing of time.

He begged to be forgiven for his desertion and this forgiveness she readily gave, saying she had always loved him. They talked contentedly throughout the evening and retired to their old bedroom to enjoy again the delights of the early years of their marriage. In the morning the samurai turned towards his wife – to find a withered corpse lying beside him. He later discovered his first wife had lived alone in the house for a few months after he had left her and then died, of a broken heart it was said. The fate of the second wife is not known.

It is sometimes said that Japanese ghosts have no feet and there are many who believe this. But it appears to be a fallacy, arising from a fashion set by the artist Maruyama Okyo who lived during the latter half of the eighteenth century and painted pictures of feetless ghosts. He founded the Shijo School around 1780. The first wife of the samurai must have had feet, as he could not have failed to notice their absence when he returned to her.

Mother-love

In another typical ghost story, the spirit again was able to walk. A shopkeeper had, for a short period, a regular customer who came every evening to buy *midzu-ame*, a syrup sometimes given to young children when milk is unobtainable. The customer was a young woman, who looked ill and very pale. She never spoke, but just pointed at the midzu-ame and paid her money. The shopkeeper became curious about her habitual single purchase and followed her one night, but turned away when he saw her walk into the village cemetery. A few evenings later, instead of buying anything she beckoned the man to follow her. He felt uneasy in her silent presence, and as he went after her in the twilight he called to a few friends in

Creatures and Spirits

the street to come along too. They all went after the woman into the cemetery, for that was where she led them.

On reaching a tomb at the far end the woman vanished, but the men were more startled by the sound of a baby crying from within. Quickly they got lights and opened up the grave. The corpse of the woman was lying there and by it was a child a few weeks old. The explanation given for this tale of mother-love is that the woman was buried while her unborn child still lived. After the child's birth the woman's spirit fed it until such time as she could ensure it would be cared for by its fellow mortals.

The wronged servant girl

Lafcadio Hearn identifies the Akasaka district in Tokyo as the setting

Left: statue of Jizo. The staff is missing. Wood, Kamakura period. William Rockhill Nelson Gallery of Art, Kansas City.

Right: Juichimen Kwannon – Kwannon with eleven faces – in the Toshodai-ji Temple in Nara.

for a ghost story in the nineteenth century. A man was walking home one night when he came across a young girl, alone, crouching by the road and crying aloud. Thinking she might have been abandoned by her lover and was contemplating suicide for that or some other reason (there was a moat nearby, a popular place for those wishing to end their lives), he paused and asked if he could be of assistance to her. She got up but did not face him, and continued to sob. He gently turned her round and saw that her face did not have features at all: it was like the shell of an egg. Screaming from shock and fear he fled through the dark streets until he came to a small stall with a single lantern on it. A man was standing in the shadows, evidently about to go home having sold his wares. The stall holder asked him why he ran so fast. Was he being chased by thieves perhaps? When the man had pulled himself together he related his frightening experience, glad to have found someone to whom he could unburden

The young Yoshitsune being taught the warrior arts by the tengu. He put the lessons to good use with his companion Benkei in the Minamoto cause. Print by Kuniyoshi. Victoria and Albert Museum.

himself. The stall holder moved into the light of the lantern and
the already terrified man saw that he, too, was utterly without
facial features.

The faceless girl ghost had not committed suicide, but there was a
servant girl who had. She was employed by a samurai who had an
heirloom taking the form of ten beautiful and precious porcelain plates.
His wife, having inadvertently broken one of these, threw the pieces
down the well on her husband's property. Moreover, to avoid the
inevitable wrath of her husband, she blamed the servant for stealing
the plate from the set. In vain the girl pleaded innocence and
finally, in total despair, she killed herself close to the well into
which her mistress had, unknown to the maid, tossed the fragments
of porcelain.

Thereafter the girl's ghost appeared each night, counting up to
the figure nine, and then instead of pronouncing the number ten,
breaking into a fearful wail. Eventually the samurai and his wife
(one likes to think she had confessed her deception and slander) were
rescued from the disturbance caused by the unhappy spirit by a
courageous friend who waited by the well for the punctual appearance
of the spirit. As the apparition said 'nine' he interjected the
following numeral. In this way the ghost was laid forever. This story,
and there are other versions of it, was one of the artist Hokusai's
favourite themes.

Plates and bowls are objects which appear frequently in the legends
from Japan. There is a story of a badger who lent such utensils, as
did a kappa in another story. A further ghost story again involves
a broken plate, a servant girl and a well. A household were preparing
for the New Year celebrations and, as was the custom in the family,
a fish salad was set out on a plate of great age and value. The maid
accidentally smashed the dish by dropping it. The master of the
household was as angry as the samurai in the previous story, and the
distress of the maid over the mishap was so overwhelming that she
drowned herself in a well. The feelings of the man over this are not
revealed but remorse must surely have been among them. For
several years afterwards blood was found in the fish salad served at
the New Year. The number of times this happened is not recorded –
perhaps the man allowed fish salad to be served as a form of self-
punishment. But after a period, that delicacy was very sensibly not
served again on New Year's Day.

A temple ghost

Everyone knows the eerie feeling engendered when a group of people
regale each other with ghost stories. Some tales told in Japan suggest
that this eeriness is sometimes enhanced to the extent that a group
may actually expect an evil happening as a result of their yarns.
One example concerns a temple novice who invited friends to a story-
telling session. They all lit candles in another room for each narrative
to be told. After each tale, the teller was to go out alone and
extinguish a candle, starting with the most frightened of the
narrators. After all the candles had been blown out and the stories
told, everyone went home with the exception of two guests.

One of them awoke and saw a ghost remove the novice, by picking
him up, bedding, pillow and all. The spectre then returned and in
the same manner took the other guest from the sleeping chamber.
The solitary watcher called out, but there was no answer to his cries.
Sleepless with terror he remained there all night and as dawn broke
he fled the place.

When he had recovered from his initial shock and sorrow, he
regularly visited the temple where his vanished host had been a
novice and prayed that further disaster would not befall the precincts.
Every time he made this pious visit he met a girl on the way back.

In due course he first courted and later married her. They had been man and wife for a considerable period when he went into their kitchen one evening and saw her blowing up the fire. Her face was that of the temple ghost.

Immediately he recalled that it was the anniversary of the story-telling evening. In fear he cried out, and he remembered too that since his marriage he had stopped his regular visits to the temple. Only disaster could follow his negligence. His wife lifted her head. There had been no mistake. She was indeed the unearthly being he had seen before. She came towards him, as he stood rooted to the spot, and breathed upon him. The story concludes with his immediate death.

Unnatural death, such as death by violence or by drowning, can

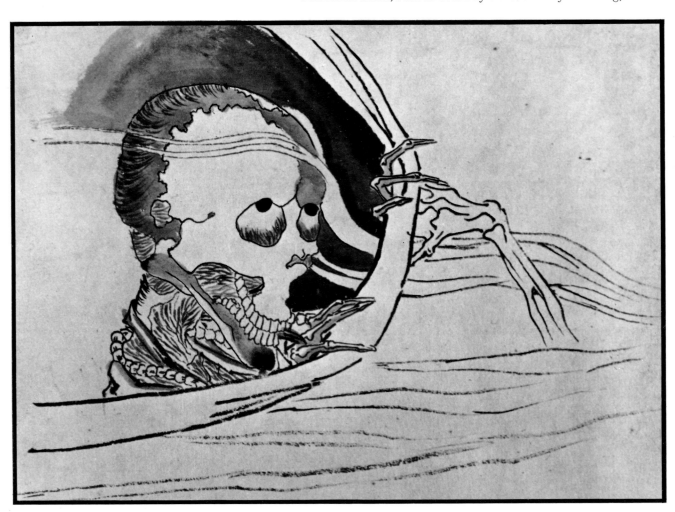

be the cause of a resentful spirit haunting its former companions. To prevent this, services are held to ease the anguish of the spirit which left its body without peace. It is claimed that a spirit, even if the death is a natural one, lingers in its lifetime abode for as long as thirty-three years. At least a proportion of the ghost or spirit stories told in this and other chapters clearly relate to spirits tormented by unease, grief or vengeance.

Malice thwarted

One tale describes a method used to avoid hauntings by a vengeful spirit, other than by religious ceremonies concerned with the burial of the dead or the honouring of the departed spirit. A man was sentenced to death by beheading. As he was placed upon the ground, firmly wedged into position with stone-filled sacks so that he could not move, he pleaded for mercy, saying the crimes

Left: head of a ghost. Painting by Hokusai. Victoria and Albert Museum.

Right: typical representation of an oni.

of which he had been convicted had been committed unwittingly. He admitted to stupidity but not to malice. He also claimed that if the sentence were carried out he would become a spirit bearing a grudge and would seek and gain retribution from his executioners. Those gathered around were much alarmed by this prognostication, but the samurai in charge remained calm. He obtained from the prisoner a promise to give a sign of his intention to take vengeance immediately after his death and the man, realising that mercy would not be given, readily gave his word. The samurai pointed to a stepping-stone directly in front of the prostrate victim (the place of execution was, strangely enough, a formal garden) and told him to try and bite it after death as a sign that his spirit would indeed be an angry one. The frantic man swore he would do this. The samurai drew his sword and with a swift, single blow severed the head from the body. The head rolled and then bounced towards the stone, seized it with its teeth, and then toppled to a standstill. The horrified watchers begged the samurai to cause a service to be held at once to ease the spirit of the man, but he explained that in this case such a course would be unnecessary. He claimed that only the last thoughts or desires of a dying person likely to become a restless spirit were of danger to those who live. This man's final thoughts had been entirely directed towards the sign of the vengeance he would bring, rather than the vengeance itself. All his ultimate living energies were directed towards the stone and the biting of it. The tale ends there, for the man never appeared in ghostly form to frighten or bewilder.

Buried treasure

Many Japanese stories concern the link between dreams and the supernatural. A couple of peddlars while resting together on a beach talked a while, until one fell asleep. As his companion slept, the other saw a fly come from the sleeping man's nose, fly in the direction of the island of Sado and, some time after, return and creep into the sleeper's nostril, at which point he awoke. No mention of the fly was made, but the man who had slept told his friend how he had dreamed of a fly which had informed him of buried treasure under a white camellia tree on Sado, in the garden of a rich man.

The dreamer took money for the sale or relating of this dream, and when their ways parted the other peddlar went to Sado. He knew the dreamer would not do likewise for, by accepting money, he had forfeited his ownership of the dream. The peddlar obtained garden employment on the island from a wealthy man there, but the camellias in his care all bore coloured blooms that spring. However, he did not lose hope and remained another year working for the rich man. His confidence and patience and his desire for worldly wealth were rewarded. The following spring, one of the camellia trees in the garden was laden with white blooms, and under it the peddlar turned gardener found a jar containing much gold. He remained in his master's employment for a while longer and then went his way, not to become a peddlar again but to enjoy the luxuries his dream investment had brought him.

Virtue rewarded

In another story, two men told each other their dreams. One dreamed of good fortune coming to him from above and the other dreamed it would come to him from the earth. The man who dreamed luck would come to him from heaven found a container in his field when digging and in it were golden coins. Such was his honesty that he left it where it was and went and told his fellow dreamer about it, saying the treasure surely belonged to him since he it was who had dreamed that good fortune would come from the

Creatures and Spirits

earth. The other man went to the place, found the buried container and took it home.

But when he opened it the gold was not there: it had become a twisting mass of snakes. The man hurried in fury to his friend's house and saw him and his wife sitting by the fire, in obvious contentment. He climbed up onto the roof and through an opening poured the contents of the container down on the man who had apparently misinformed him. But the snakes had changed back into gold, and the man who had dreamed of fortune from above received a cascade of money from the roof of his own house.

Hoichi's ordeal

The famous story of Hoichi also concerns a dream. Or maybe it was

Left: a mourning Bird Man lamenting the death of Buddha. It closely resembles portrayals of the mythological tengu. Clay, between 710 and 794. Seattle Art Museum.

Right: Umi Bozu, the giant ghost Sea Priest or Monk, who rises from the depths to frighten voyagers. Print by Kuniyoshi. Victoria and Albert Museum.

not all a dream. Hoichi is described as a priest and also a poor man skilled with the biwa, Benten's favourite instrument. He was known to be blind and musical, and he lived at the Amidaji Temple in Shimonoseki, at the extreme south-western tip of Honshu. This temple was built to appease the spirits of the Taira clan who perished at the Battle of Dannoura in the Straits of Shimonoseki which separate Honshu from Kyushu. These spirits appeared in the form of moving lights on the sea and along the coasts. Certain crabs are also supposed to be Taira wraiths and are in general another way in which the spirits of the unhappy dead show themselves. The blind biwa player was particularly gifted in his own accompanied rendering of the *Heike Monogatari*, the tragic story of the Taira clan and their final defeat which involved the death of the infant Emperor Antoku.

One night the chief priest of the temple was out and as Hoichi sat on the verandah he heard footsteps approaching, the noise indicating that their owner was dressed in armour. The visitor addressed Hoichi by name and said he was in the service of a daimyo who, escorted by many retainers, was visiting the area, in particular the scene of the Battle of Dannoura. Obviously the visitor to the temple was a samurai, wearing full battle array. The samurai said he had been commanded to bring Hoichi to the place where the company were assembled in order that they might hear his rendering of the *Heike Monogatari*. Much flattered by this request, Hoichi allowed himself to be led away from the temple. He was unable to ascertain where he was being taken and his guide was silent, but on passing through a large gate Hoichi was greeted by a woman who led him to a seat and invited him to begin his recitation, accompanying himself on the biwa. Hoichi was aware of being in a large, crowded room with an audience fully appreciative of his performance. The armoured samurai took him back to the temple after the woman had informed him that the daimyo had expressed a wish to hear Hoichi repeat the performance nightly during his week's stay in Shimonoseki, with the proviso that the blind man

Right: the ghost of Emperor Sutoku (1124-41) racing across a stormy sea from his rock of exile. Print by Kuniyoshi. Victoria and Albert Museum.

A legendary ghostly scene of the spirit of a hero named Yoshihiro appearing at Nunobiki Falls. Victoria and Albert Museum.

should not tell anyone about it, since he did not wish his tour of the area to be known locally. The same sequence of events followed the next night, with the exception that one of the acolytes in the temple noticed Hoichi's absence, and in the morning the priest in charge asked Hoichi where he had been.

The blind man, remembering the woman's request, gave an evasive answer. Fearing for the safety of the sightless man, the priest asked to be notified at once if Hoichi were seen to be out of the temple. Naturally enough, that third night his room was found to be empty and a search of the neighbourhood was immediately started with some urgency, because it was a stormy night and raining hard.

Hoichi was found, sitting on the memorial stone to the Emperor Antoku in the temple cemetery, surrounded by ghostly lights, playing on his biwa and reciting, oblivious to his surroundings and the drenching rain. He was enraged at being interrupted, protesting that the great company for whom he performed must be indignant, too. After a struggle Hoichi was taken back to the temple, calmed and put to bed. It was explained to him where he had been found. Undoubtedly he was the human victim of the Taira spirits. Was the voice of the unknown woman the spirit of the dead child-emperor's mother, or grandmother? Or had it been just a dream that had caused Hoichi to walk in his sleep for three nights in succession?

In order to protect Hoichi from further manifestations the priest instructed his acolytes to cover Hoichi's body with protective Buddhist texts, even to the soles of his feet and the palms of his hands. He himself was told to sit on the verandah and to sit still and silent if approached, as though in deep meditation: only thus could he escape harm.

That night he heard the footsteps of the samurai, the now familiar rattle of armour and then the voice, calling his name. Hoichi neither moved nor answered. Then he heard the voice, raised in resentment, complaining that only Hoichi's ears and his biwa were visible. The samurai went on that he must take these ears back to his master to prove that he had attempted to obey his orders. Hoichi was then silently subjected to the torture of having his ears wrenched from his head, and he was in an unconscious state when the chief priest and temple attendants found him. It was discovered that the acolytes had omitted his ears when carrying out their instructions with the texts. Hoichi recovered from his shock and wounds and from that time on bore the somewhat obvious name of Hoichi the Earless.

The restless Taira ghosts may also be seen in the sea. Tomomori is reputed to have been seen walking the waves, dragging a ship's anchor after him. He was the Taira hero who broke the news of the impending defeat to the Emperor Antoku's mother, whereupon she took the death leap with her son in her arms. And there is a story, too, of how a multitude of Taira ghosts (the casualties at the battle were heavy) surrounded a ship in which Yoshitsune and Benkei were travelling, some time after the Minamoto victory. Benkei dispersed the throng by reciting Buddhist prayers and holding a rosary.

Lafcadio Hearn, who wrote so much about the supernatural in Japan, tells of other ghosts of the drowned, not necessarily Taira ones, who call out for a bucket from passing ships. It is dangerous to refuse such requests, but it is essential to remove the bottom of the bucket before giving it to the spirit. Otherwise the ghost will fill the bucket with water and sink the ship. Hearn does not say what penalty the ghost will exact from human voyagers if no bucket is handed to them. One feels that Benkei's solution to the haunting of the Taira spirits to which he and his master were subjected was probably the best – certainly it was efficacious.

Four of the twenty-nine pictures of ghosts and mythical creatures on a scroll entitled Bakemonojin or Compendium of Ghosts. One of these creatures is a kappa coming out of its pool. Colour wash and ink. Dated 1788. Museum für Völkerkunde, Vienna.

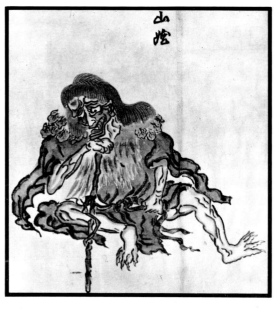

HEROES AND HEROINES

A monstrous spectral cat haunts a young man.
Print by Kunisada. Victoria and Albert Museum.

The term hero was applied from earliest times to one possessed
with superhuman strength and courage and favoured by the gods.
Indeed many of the ancient Japanese heroes were gods themselves,
including Susano, Oh-kuni-nushi and his little friend Suku-na-biko
or Small Renown Man. Later the word applied to those valiant in
battle, noble in their aims and chivalrous in their actions. Japanese
heroes are similar to the heroes of other countries, but there are some
differences. They were, of course, influenced by their environment:
as an island people they fought on the sea as well as on the land.
Shintoism nurtured a patriotism coupled with devotion to an
emperor of divine origin, and Buddhism encouraged the Japanese
code of chivalry known as Bushido. The family is important, too,

Right: the pagoda at the Muro-ji Temple in Nara. The temple was founded in 676 and rebuilt by Kobo Daishi in 824. He is said to have carved the main image in the temple, but such legends about him abound.

A samurai riding beneath a cherry tree in bloom. Kakemono. Museum für Völkerkunde, Vienna.

and there are many examples of filial piety. Many heroes committed *hara-kiri*, ceremonial self-disembowelment, to maintain family honour, to expiate a fault or even to follow a master.

The hero – the word is used in its modern sense – of the Russo-Japanese War (1904–5), General Count Nogi, committed hara-kiri, as did his wife, following the death of Emperor Meiji in 1912. Various theories for this sacrifice were put forward at the time, but it is accepted that he wished to serve his monarch in death as he had done in life. He is thus a hero in the old and Japanese meaning. The *Kamikaze* (the word means divine wind) or suicide pilots of the Second World War were heroes of this type, and undoubtedly in time that war will produce its legendary heroes, as all wars do.

In 1932 three private soldiers of the Imperial Army in Shanghai carried a lighted explosive bomb to an enemy barbed wire defensive position. They blew up the section and died, as they knew they would. They are known as the Three Heroes of Chapei or The Human Bomb. They belong to history – their courage is already passing into legend.

The ferocity and brutalities of the Second World War have no place here, but the armies of Japan believed, as their forebears had down the centuries, that it is better to die by one's own hand in battle if one cannot die for one's cause at the hand of the enemy. To be taken prisoner is without honour and without heroism.

Physical courage is admired in Japan as much as anywhere else. Suicide for the reasons of Bushido is looked upon with sorrow, as in the West, but it is also regarded as a valiant death when the motive is honourable. Another factor which is possibly involved in the Japanese conception of heroism is *giri*. It is difficult to translate this idea. It means literally a self-imposed moral obligation with a sentimental impulse. In at least some of the heroic and other myths and legends, giri is present.

Jimmu Tenno, the first emperor, was also the first demi-god who was a human hero. With the Japanese respect for old age perhaps his exploits gain a certain lustre by his longevity, for he is said to have lived to the age of one hundred and thirty-seven.

Momotaro

The Small Renown Man was a god—and a tiny one. He is a hero for his nobility of purpose rather than for his prowess in battle. Momotaro combines the two virtues. He came into being in a peach. A childless couple found the peach floating down a mountain stream and when they took it home and opened it, there was a perfectly formed minute human boy. They named him Momotaro, which means peach child, but it has been rather coyly translated as Little Peachling. The couple regarded him as their own, and he grew up to be both dutiful and brave. The people of the area were being terrorised by a number of oni which inhabited an island and were making raids on the mainland to steal its treasures.

Momotaro at the age of fifteen resolved to act. Before setting off on his self-imposed mission, his foster-mother gave him some rice cakes. On the way he met a dog, a pheasant and a monkey in that order. They were all able to converse with him and with each other and in turn they joined him on his expedition, in each case in return for a rice cake. When the quartet reached the coast, they found a boat and had an uneventful voyage to the island of the oni.

On landing they came across some girls who had been kidnapped and raped by marauding oni and held captive on the island. Momotaro told them he would return them safely to their families on the mainland when he had destroyed their captors.

With his bird and animal friends he attacked the oni castle and killed all the supernatural inhabitants, the leader being slain by

Yorimitsu and his henchmen killing a giant.
Print by Kuniyoshi. Victoria and Albert Museum.

Momotaro himself in a duel. They then released all the human prisoners they found in the castle, fetched the girls they had met on landing, and also filled their boat with the treasures stolen by the oni. The return voyage was without incident and the rescued were duly escorted to their homes and the treasure returned to its owners. There was enough of the oni loot left for Momotaro to ensure that his foster-parents lived in comfort for the rest of their lives. It would appear that the dog, the pheasant and the monkey sought only the glory of helping the youthful hero, as, apart from a rice cake each, they gained nothing from the expedition.

Issun Boshi
Issun Boshi was another tiny hero. His name means Little One Inch.

Heroes and Heroines

He had a normal birth following the usual pregnancy period (heroes are often long in the womb) after his parents had been married many years without children. Before his conception they had prayed at their local shrine for a child, even if it should be only the size of the end of a finger. The gods took their prayer literally.

As in the case of Momotaro, the most famous story about Issun Boshi begins when he reached the age of fifteen. It would seem that Momotaro had attained normal size by then, but Issun Boshi was still tiny. He expressed a wish to visit the capital, Kyoto at the time. His parents gave him a rice bowl, a pair of chopsticks and a needle to use as a sword, stuck in a scabbard made of a hollow straw. He had to make the journey partly by river, and he floated down in his lacquer rice bowl, using the chopsticks to steer it.

In spite of his diminutive size, Issun Boshi was not trampled on in the city and in due course was able to enter the service of a noble family. He was clever and hard working and endeared himself to the household, particularly to the daughter of the house. After several years had passed, he accompanied her one day to pray at the temple dedicated to the goddess Kwannon. On the way, two giant oni barred the way and Issun Boshi leapt about to try and distract their attention from the girl. One of the oni spotted him, picked him up and swallowed him. Immediately the little youth drew his needle sword and began to stab the oni's stomach. Then he worked his way up into the gullet, wielding his sword as he climbed. So painful was this for the oni that it spat Issun Boshi out as soon as it could. The other oni then picked him up, but the tiny fellow jumped into its eye and there put his miniature sword to good use. As the devils took flight, the hero of the story tumbled, unhurt, to the ground.

In their escape one of the oni dropped a mallet, which the girl recognised as being lucky – an object able to grant wishes. Daikoku, the god of Wealth and one of the seven gods of Good Fortune or Luck, is often depicted holding such a mallet. Together the girl and the little young man struck the mallet on the ground and wished. Immediately Issun Boshi became of normal size, dressed as a samurai, the bearing and manner of which station he had already shown.

When they returned, the father of the girl gladly allowed the couple to marry. The pair certainly deserved the luck of the dropped mallet. Issun Boshi's life continued less hazardously, but he proved himself to be well endowed with the samurai spirit, and as well as being a good husband he brought his parents to Kyoto and cared for them in their old age. He and Momotaro had much in common.

Kintaro
Kintaro was known for his tremendous physical strength and loyalty.

A Ryobu Shinto torii at the Sanno Temple in the Nagata district of Tokyo. Painting by Hiroshige (1797-1858). Victoria and Albert Museum.

Right: Yorimitsu, also known as Raiko, was an early Minamoto hero with four lieutenants, one of whom was Tsuna. This brave man undertook to keep guard at the Rashomon Gate in Kyoto when the demon Ibaraki was understood to be haunting it. Just before dawn he felt an unearthly hand on the back of his head and made a quick back slash with his sword. He then discovered he had cut off Ibaraki's huge and hairy arm and clawed hand. This tale of Tsuna ends by the demon getting its arm back by changing itself temporarily into the form of Tsuna's old nurse. The scene at the Rashomon Gate is shown. Print by Kuniyoshi. Victoria and Albert Museum.

Kintaro's mother was one of the mountain spirits known as Yama-uba. She has also been described as a mortal, devoted to her warrior husband who was wrongfully banished from court. As Yama-uba, she was the warrior's mistress. Kintaro was a posthumous child and was brought up in a mountain retreat, with only his mother and animals as his companions. Apparently he was a beautiful child, with golden skin. He was, as a small boy, strong to the extent of being able to uproot trees with only one hand.

To wrestle with a bear was merely an exercise, involving no danger for the child. Apart from his strength, Kintaro showed a certain wisdom in his childhood, for he used to adjudicate when his animal friends tussled together to test their strength, though there is no record of Kintaro being an onlooker of an animal fight to the death. His strength was eventually discovered and he was taken to the court at Kyoto where, it is believed, he eventually became a retainer of Yorimitsu, an early leader of the Minamoto clan. Eventually Kintaro vindicated his father's name and in manhood became a warrior too.

Raiko, or Yorimitsu

Raiko was served in his Minamoto leadership by four lieutenants. One of Raiko's exploits was to defeat a small band of giant oni which had been attacking women in the mountains. The leader of this group lived off human blood and was also a nimble swordsman.

Heroes and Heroines

Raiko, or Yorimitsu, the name more generally used, being harried by the Earth Spider. As is so often the case, Yorimitsu is shown with his four companions, although at this point of the story they are unaware of their master's torment. Print by Kuniyoshi. Victoria and Albert Museum.

Raiko and his henchmen were charged to rid the place of these creatures. Not for the first time a hero discharged his duty by cunning as well as valour. Disguised as a band of wandering priests and fully armed under their robes, they went to the hidden mountain fortress of their intended victims and offered them a magic drink. The giants were not aware of the priests' identity and thoroughly enjoyed the drink and the entertainment of impromptu dancing which Raiko put on for them. When the magic drink had had its inebriating effect (perhaps because of their particular oni nature, ordinary sake would not have had the same result), the warriors discarded their priestly robes and in full armour beheaded the creatures. The vampire leader was so enraged by this indignity that

his severed head tried to attack Raiko. But the Minamoto warriors won the day and also rescued a number of captive women whom they found near the oni's hiding place in the mountain forest.

One of the several stories told of Raiko concerns the time he became ill. He lived in considerable comfort in a mansion in Kyoto, with numerous servants. He did not think it strange, therefore, that at midnight his medicine was brought to him by a youth whom he did not know. However, as his illness worsened, he began to suspect this youth of either poisoning him or, worse, of having evil powers. One night he suddenly attacked the boy, who fled yelling from the room, throwing an outsize and sticky spider's web at Raiko. Although he cut through it with his sword, it continued to entwine the invalid.

One of Raiko's lieutenants heard the commotion. Rushing to his master's aid, he met the strange youth in the passage, and he too was covered with a web of supernatural quality. The so-called servant was eventually discovered in a cave in his real guise of a goblin spider, suffering from the sword cut which Raiko had given him from the sick-bed. The phantom creature was killed and Raiko not only recovered immediately from the undiagnosed disease, but the glutinous spider webs disintegrated, releasing Raiko and his staunch lieutenant.

Tawara Toda

Another hero, Tawara Toda, is said to belong to the eleventh century, but so surrounded by magic are the stories about him that one cannot but wonder whether he ever lived. In legend, at least, he was a man of bravery and honour. The setting of one of the stories about him is Lake Biwa, which features so often in Japanese mythology. Tawara Toda was crossing a bridge over the river leading out of the lake when he saw a hideous and vast serpent lying in his way. Such was his courage – some might say foolhardiness – that he made no attempt to kill it, but merely climbed over its scaly body and went his way. It was lying passively on the bridge; perhaps if it had shown any aggressiveness Tawara Toda would have acted differently.

At this point the renderings of the story vary. In one version he was later visited at his home by a young woman who revealed herself to be the daughter of the Dragon King, saying that in her true form she had been the serpent he had passed so unconcernedly on the bridge. Another version states that, having reached the other side of the river, Tawara Toda turned to look back, and instead of the serpent lying where he had left it there was a man-like being, wearing a crown with a small serpent on it. This stranger said he was the Dragon King himself. He claimed to have taken the shape of the creature in order to find a human brave enough to undertake a task which could be performed only by a mortal. The versions then converge again, for Tawara Toda was invited to slay a gigantic and magical centipede which had been threatening the realm of the Dragon King. The centipede was so huge that it covered a mountain: balls of fire glowed in its head and all its hundred feet were illuminated. The human hero was a fine archer, but though his first two arrows aimed at the fire balls each found their mark, the creature appeared to be unhurt. Saliva is said to have magical lethal properties on occasion. Tawara Toda remembered this and put it to the test. He licked the head of his third arrow and took aim. The centipede died as the arrow hit it.

After this triumph Tawara Toda was entertained in the Dragon King's palace below Lake Biwa. (Entertainment is a quite usual sequel to deeds of prowess: Raiko was given a feast after he and his retainers had rescued the girls from the oni.) A sumptuous feast was provided, music played and the whole occasion was magnificent. As a final act of gratitude, the Dragon King gave his human guest not his daughter in marriage, as might be expected in this type of heroic tale, but supernatural gifts: a bag of rice, the contents of which never had to be replenished however much was taken from it; a roll of silk cloth which again was self-replenishing as lengths were cut from it; a cooking pot which heated without the use of fire; and a bell, long hidden under the waters of the lake. Only the bell was without magic, and this gift Tawara Toda gave to a local temple. One likes to think he did so to commemorate the ensured safety of the Dragon King's domain now the centipede was dead, rather than to dispose of an object that, compared with his other presents, was mundane indeed.

Tawara Toda's name can be translated as Lord Toda of the Rice-bale or My Lord Bag of Rice. The English versions of the various stories about him generally use the latter as a title. Hidesato is another name given to this hero.

93

Right: an ancient dance mask representing an old man. The eyes are white and the lips red. Museum für Völkerkunde, Vienna.

Below: Yoshitsune in a ship with his retainers. Print by Kuniyoshi. Victoria and Albert Museum.

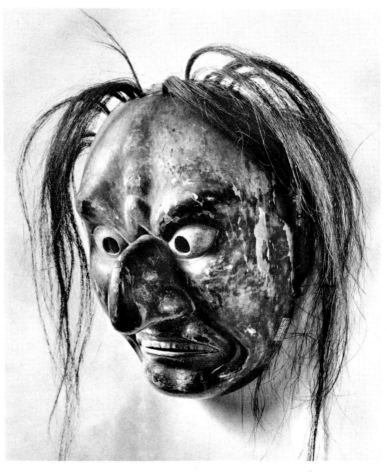

94

Tametomo belongs to the twelfth century and has appeared before as one of the Minamoto heroes. Possibly because his nephew Yoshitsune had a retainer called Benkei, of whom so much has been written and told, Tametomo has comparatively few legends surrounding him. One remarkable fact about him was that when he was exiled one of the various tortures inflicted on him was to have the sinews of his arm cut. In spite of this, he was later able to sink an enemy ship with a single arrow. It is really as a great archer and patriot that Tametomo is known.

Benkei and Yoshitsune

Oni, phantom creatures and serpents were almost always the vanquished enemies of heroes, but the tengu were very much on the side of Yoshitsune and Benkei. According to a document in the Nagami Shrine, Honjo-mura, the daughter of a samurai, was born on 5 May 1129 and named Benkichi. In 1147 she went to Nagami and three years later conceived a child there by a tengu. Her son, Benkei, was born thirteen months later – another hero long in the womb – with a complete set of teeth and long hair. There is a legend that in his early youth he lived with his mother on an island called Benkeijima off the Nohara coast in Honjo-mura. Apparently, he was a tiresome child and was abandoned there for his viciousness. The island is connected to the mainland by a narrow sandy path. This path is reputed to have been made by the child who carried sand in the sleeves and skirt of his garment in order to make an escape route from the island.

He must have been reconciled with his mother, for it is also told that after her death, when he was seventeen years old, he caused her to be enshrined as the goddess Benkichi at Nagami. It is further said that on the island, as a small boy, he used to play with tengu. But Benkei is claimed to be a priest's son as well as the child of a tengu. He has been described as being ten feet tall in manhood, with the strength of a hundred men and able to run as fast as the wind. His meeting with Yoshitsune on the Gojo Bridge in Kyoto has been retold times without number, and there is a Noh drama about it, probably dating from the fifteenth century. In order to relate that story again, it is necessary to go back to Tametomo's nephew, Yoshitsune.

As a child and young man, this hero of the Minamoto clan was known by the name of Ushiwaka, in the same manner as Yorimitsu was at one period of is life known as Raiko. After the young Ushiwaka and his two brothers had been reluctantly spared from death by the Tairas following a Minamoto defeat, Ushiwaka was sent alone to a monastery where the monks looked after him and where he helped them in some of their duties. But he came of fighting stock and even as a little boy vowed to bring retribution on the Tairas for the defeat they had inflicted on his family. He used to go out on the mountain side at night and practice swordsmanship with a wooden toy sword he had made himself. The principal tengu took pity on the boy. One night it appeared to him and asked him about his nightly secret visits to the woods. The tengu was impressed by the child's determination and it also approved of the Minamoto clan. It arranged for the tengu's retainers, the Leaflet tengu, to teach Ushiwaka not only swordsmanship, but strategy and tactics as well. Thus in his childhood and youth Ushiwaka learned the warrior arts from the supernatural world, and by the time he became a man and was known as Yoshitsune, his exploits were such that his prowess in battle had a good deal of the supernatural about it. Whether Benkei was the child of a tengu or not, the fact that he is supposed to have had tengu companions in his childhood too is something the two heroes had in common. The tale

of their meeting on the Gojo Bridge is the first of the legends
in which they both feature: after that meeting there are no separate
stories about either of them.

Ushiwaka was in his middle teens, well trained in the warrior arts
and a pious youth when he heard of a soldier-monk named Benkei.
This man had made a reputation for himself by attacking warriors
in order to show off his swordsmanship. Benkei collected the swords of
those he set upon to satisfy his vanity. He had been attached to the
monastery of Mount Hiei and had come to Kyoto to seek adventure
and more sword trophies.

When crossing the Gojo Bridge on his way to worship at a temple
on the other side, Ushiwaka saw the man he had heard about,
waiting there to challenge the next warrior who crossed to a fencing
bout or duel. If he was really ten feet tall he must have been formidable
indeed in appearance, dressed in his full armour. Benkei scorned
Ushiwaka, not so much for his youthfulness, but for his slight build.
However, he challenged him and tried to block his way. The tengu
training stood the boy in good stead and he quickly slipped past the
huge man standing in front of him, knocking one of Benkei's
assortment of weapons out of his hand as he did so. Benkei turned
in fury and so began the famous fight. Ushiwaka disarmed the vain
fighter and was clearly the victor of the contest. Benkei's attitude to
life changed from then on. He begged to be forgiven of the youth
who had established himself as not only more skilled in swordsmanship
but of greater honour. Benkei offered to become Ushiwaka's
servant and companion in the feud against the Tairas. This offer was
accepted, and from that first meeting Ushiwaka, Yoshitsune as he
became, and Benkei were inseparable and their names are coupled
in both history and legend.

Yoritomo, Yoshitsune's elder half-brother, was jealous of the pair,
in spite of the help they gave him against the Tairas. Eventually
Yoshitsune had to flee to the north of Japan to escape his brother
after the final victory of the Tairas. This inordinate jealousy which
Yoritomo felt against Yoshitsune seems to have bordered on insanity.
Yoshitsune had been loyalty itself to the Minamoto cause and surely
would have been helpful to his brother in the early days of the
Kamakura shogunate. But perhaps he would have been too helpful:
Yoritomo had much of the dictator in him. Legend says that
Yoshitsune was finally killed by Yoritomo's minions, that his head
was preserved in sake and sent back to Yoritomo in Kamakura, and
that Benkei died in the attempted defence of his master. Another
version of their end is that they committed hara-kiri when they saw
there was no hope of surviving the attack on them organised by
Yoritomo, and yet another version, as has been related earlier, has
Yoshitsune going to Yezo (Hokkaido) and then to the mainland of
Asia. Presumably Benkei went with him. But it is equally accepted
that Benkei died for his master, an appropriate ending to the life
of a man who was nicknamed Oni-waka or 'Devil Youth' in his
childhood for his violence and who, through his meeting with the
young Yoshitsune, became a warrior of loyal gallantry, an attribute
enhanced by his supernatural strength.

Yoritomo, in spite of his inhuman cruelty and unnatural jealousy
of his brother, must be counted as a hero. Not only was he the first
shogun but he was the victor of the Battle of Dannoura, the sea
engagement at which the Taira clan were finally annihilated. After
he had established his administration in Kamakura, he founded a
system of government through military governors, and military
feudalism was the accepted pattern for years to come. Whatever may
be thought of him, he did command devotion among his retainers,
one of whom was Asahina Saburo who certainly comes into the classic
category of hero. Often he is depicted as being able to hurl rocks with

Heroes and Heroines

superhuman strength, and he is also said to have been able to swim with a live shark under each arm.

The Taira side had their heroes, too. Kagekiyo also belonged to the latter part of the twelfth century. He was one of many who attempted to kill Yoritomo (who died of natural causes at a considerable age, in spite of a life devoted to fighting and intrigue). When the final defeat of the Tairas came, Kagekiyo put out his own eyes rather than look upon the Minamoto victory.

Atsumori and Kumagai

Before the Battle of Dannoura there was a land battle near Kobe, at Ichi-no-tani. Yoshitsune and Benkei were its victors, and Benkei suggested that the castle held by the Tairas should be stormed from

Left: Yegara-no-Heida killing Uwabami, a giant serpent reputed to be able to swallow a man on horseback in a single gulp. Print by Shuntei. Victoria and Albert Museum.

Right: Daikoku, one of the Seven Gods of Luck, shaves the elongated head of another of the Seven, Fukurokuju. Ink and colour wash, painted during the late seventeenth or eighteenth century. Seattle Art Museum.

the steep mountain above and behind it. Atsumori was a young hero on the Taira side at this encounter. He was only sixteen years of age, and he fought like a man. He was the nephew of the Taira leader, Kiyomori. When the Battle of Ichi-no-tani was over and the Taira forces had fled, Atsumori was left in the castle. He killed three Minamoto warriors and then hurried to the beach. But the Taira forces had either been killed or had taken to their boats. A Minamoto general, named Kumagai, came up and mocked the Taira soldier for being alone there. For all his youth Atsumori drew his sword and a duel was fought. Kumagai's superior strength and experience was decisive and he commanded Atsumori to take off his helmet before being beheaded.

Kumagai then saw he had fought with a boy. His own son had been killed earlier that day, and when he learned from the youth who he was, he was loath to carry out the execution. Atsumori did not ask for mercy, and perhaps because by this time the Minamoto forces under Kumagai's command were reaching the beach, he received none. Kumagai was not the first heroic character to experience such a temptation, and he was certainly not the last. But his followers did not see him show leniency to an enemy. After he had killed Atsumori, he discarded his knightly apparel (the sight of his own forces did not deter him from this) and when the sea

Right: flower offerings and unfavourable mikuji *(horoscopes) before the Bishamon altar at the Todai-ji Temple in Nara.*

Far right: Miyajima, also known as Itsukushima, is sacred to three Shinto goddesses, daughters of Susano, the eldest of whom was Itsukushima-Hime. It is believed that the present temple is on the site of one built during the reign of Empress Suiko (593-628), but all records were burnt in the sixteenth century. The torii in the sea in front of the temple is a favourite subject with artists and photographers.

battle which followed in the Straits of Shimonoseki had been fought and won, Kumagai became a monk in Kyoto. He also ensured that Atsumori's head was given to the boy's father – an act, curiously enough, of kindness in this instance.

Just before the Ashikaga shogunate was established, the Emperor Go-Daigo had a general who proved to be loyal to him at a time when all others deserted him. The most notable among his disloyal followers was Takauji Ashikaga, a member of a fighting family of Minamoto descent. In 1333 the faithful general, Yoshisada by name, attacked Kamakura. The defences proved to be impregnable, and the sea approach was well guarded by the forces of the Hojo regent. An abnormally low tide could explain Yoshisada's eventual encirclement of the city. But the general climbed a cliff and prayed for the help of the god of the Sea. As an offering to the deity he tossed his sword away, down the slope into the water – an act no

fighting man does lightly. The sea is reputed to have instantly
withdrawn a mile and a half. Certainly there was plenty of room for
manoeuvre before the final victory. The defending Hojo regent
acted with heroism on this occasion, too, for he committed
hara-kiri. The Ashikaga government came into power shortly after
this critical period.

The robber Ishikawa Goyemon, who lived at the end of the sixteenth
century, was said to have the physical power of thirty men. His
crimes caught up with him and he was sentenced to be boiled
in oil together with his son. There was gallantry about the man, for
he was able to compose a poem before his execution, the gist of which
is that even if the stones in the river beds and the sand by the sea
cease to be, the profession of robbery will never die. The actual death
sentence was carried out in a dry river bed near Kyoto, as
presumably Ishikawa Goyemon knew it would be.

99

The Forty-Seven Ronin

The Forty-Seven Ronin – heroes all of them – belong to the early
eighteenth century and since then their story has caught the popular
imagination to the extent of being filmed. In 1702, during the
Tokugawa shogunate, two daimyo were chosen by the shogun to
entertain in Yedo an embassy from the imperial court of Kyoto.
One of the shogun's officials, by the name of Kira Kozuke-no-Suke,
was given the task of teaching them the necessary ceremonial.
According to custom, the two daimyo gave him presents in return for
this instruction, but he was a churlish man and regarded the gifts as
being unworthy of his services to them. He despised the two noblemen
for their lack of knowledge of court etiquette and for what, in his
opinion, was paltry recompense for his superior knowledge. One of the

daimyo had an adviser who, realising the situation was becoming
hazardous, secretly paid Kira Kozuke-no-Suke a large sum of
money. In this way the daimyo was restored to favour. But the other
daimyo, whose name was Asano, had no such friend. Kira Kozuke-
no-Suke, in his petty-mindedness, began openly insulting this pupil's
apparent poverty and lack of learning.

    To such behaviour there could be only one answer, the preservation
of honour by the death of the shogun's official. While the two daimyo
were receiving instruction in the shogun's palace, Kira Kozuke-no-
Suke made a particularly insulting remark about Asano at which
the daimyo lost his temper and sprang at him with his dagger. There
were too many people present for the blow to be lethal, and Kira
Kozuke-no-Suke was only slightly hurt. Asano was seized by other
palace officials. The punishment for such an offence within the
precincts of the shogun's residence was to commit hara-kiri. The

Left: the Forty-Seven Ronin attack the residence of the man who had dishonoured their master. Print by Hiroshige. Victoria and Albert Museum.

Right: a mask made of bamboo and plaited paper and painted in black and red stripes. Museum für Völkerkunde, Vienna.

daimyo duly disembowelled himself with the dagger he had used in his attempt on Kira Kozuke-no-Suke's life.

Asano had forty-seven samurai retainers. After his death they had no choice but to disband and become *ronin*, masterless samurai. One of the ronin named Kuranosuke became their natural leader. For nearly a year they all acted as though their master's death called for no retribution and they were never seen together. But plans were made with the greatest care and stealth, and on the evening of 14 December 1703 the ronin stormed Kira Kozuke-no-Suke's mansion. It was snowing at the time and the attendants did not hear them coming. Kuranosuke attacked the front entrance and his sixteen-year-old son the back. After a stiff fight all the defenders were either killed or had run away, with the exception of Kira Kozuke-no-Suke. Eventually he was found hiding ignominiously in a charcoal storehouse on the premises. Kuranosuke commanded him to commit hara-kiri, but this he would not do. So Kuranosuke beheaded him, not with a clean blow from a sword, but with the dagger which his master had used when he had had the courage to kill himself as ordered. The head was taken by the forty-seven and laid on the tomb of the daimyo Asano in the grounds of Sengakuji Temple, Shiba, in the city now known as Tokyo.

The story follows its logical course: the ronin were all called upon to commit hara-kiri themselves, which they did, including Kuranosuke's boy. They were all buried together and their graves near that of Asano and such of their relics as have been preserved are revered still.

Heroines

But heroism is not a quality confined to the male sex. The legends and indeed the history of Japan include many heroines. One may doubt the veracity of some of the Empress Jingo's achievements, but one cannot doubt her heroism. And earlier still, Yamamoto Date's mistress displayed heroic behaviour. She accompanied him on most of his expeditions and finally flung herself to the mercies of the sea gods in order to stop the tempest which threatened her lover's ship. Kiyomori's daughter, the mother of the infant emperor Antoku, leapt into the sea carrying her son at the Battle of Dannoura, rather than allow him to fall into the hands of the Minamotos. She, too, trusted in the mercy of the gods of the sea. Her mother leapt to her death at the same time.

Kesa Gozen belonged to the twelfth century as did Emperor Antoku's mother and grandmother. She was young, beautiful and married. She and her husband lived in her mother's house. A cousin of hers, in his late teens, fell violently in love with her. She spurned the advances of the younger man and was faithful to her husband, whose duties took him away from the house often. During those troubled years, he was doubtless away fighting. The cousin tried to win Kesa Gozen's favour through her mother, and finally, such was his passion, he resorted to threatening the old lady.

At last Kesa Gozen feared so much for her mother's safety that she told her cousin she would sleep with him, but only if her husband were dead – and at his hand. She took her husband's place in their bed the night he next returned. The youth crept into the room, but the wife made no movement. She knew exactly what was in store for her. Her cousin stabbed her and in her own death she saved both her mother and her husband, and her own honour. Whether or not the husband intended to take justice upon himself is not always related, although in one version of the story he was drowned in his search for the murderer. Vengeance would seem to have been unnecessary, for the young cousin was so shocked by what he had done that he gave up all attempts at human pleasure and became a monk. He was evidently suited to that life, for eventually he became a saint, known as Mongaku Shonin.

Another heroine at the end of the twelfth century was Tora Gozen. She was a prostitute in Oiso, but gave up her trade to be with one man, Soga no Goro. He, with his elder brother Juro, attempted to kill the murderer of their father. This act of retribution happened in Yoritomo's hunting lodge near Kamakura in 1193 – after Yoritomo had become shogun. The attempt failed and Juro was killed. Goro was captured and his punishment was to be beheaded with a blunted sword. Tora Gozen was not convicted for her part in the affair. Goro's death was torment enough, and in view of her fame in her old profession there may have been ulterior motives for the clemency shown her. If that was so, it was a mistaken decision, because she renounced the world for a life of contemplation.

Terute Hime belongs to the fifteenth century. Like Tora Gozen

Heroes and Heroines

she had been a prostitute before becoming a faithful mistress. Her
lover's name was Oguri Hangwan. He was a man with enemies. On
one occasion he was lured into taking a bath with a poison in it which
gave him leprosy. Terute Hime pushed him a great distance in a
wheelbarrow from Kamakura to some hot springs where, after bathing
for a week, he recovered. In her prostitute days, she learned of a plot
to drug, rob and murder Oguri Hangwan. But she told him of the plan
and they escaped together from his house, finishing their journey
together on the back of an unbroken horse.

Faithfulness to husband or lover in the face of defeat or peril is
something all these heroines share, in some cases coupled with
loyalty to a cause. Perhaps the best exponent of the heroic qualities
in modern times is Countess Nogi, who followed the ancient traditions

*Left: Hotei, one of the Seven Gods of Luck. He is
wearing the clothes of a courtesan,
but is still recognisable by his large naked stomach.
Victoria and Albert Museum.*

*Right: the Empress Jingo, who led an expedition to
Korea and is said to have ruled in the third
century. Her son, who succeeded her, was Ojin,
later to be deified as Hachiman, the God of War.
Victoria and Albert Museum.*

of scrupulous loyalty and self-controlled valour when, with her
husband, she committed hara-kiri in their home on the night of 13
September 1912 as the Emperor Meiji's funeral procession left the
Imperial Palace in Tokyo.

One of the two Nio, guardian king, whose images
stand at temple gates to frighten off demons.
One Nio represents Indra and the other Brahma.
Hokusai school, eighteenth or nineteenth century.
Metropolitan Museum of Art, New York.

MEN AND ANIMALS

Jurojin, one of the Seven Gods of Luck. He is associated with longevity and is often shown with a crane or, as in this case, a stag. He is usually dressed as a scholar, wearing a headdress. Ink on paper, mounted as a kakemono. Museum für Völkerkunde, Vienna.

Men and Animals

Every country has its talking animal stories and Japan is no exception. Animals play an important part in both mythology and legend, not just in their own right but on account of their relationship with mortals or, in the earliest narratives, deities. The creatures can be grateful to humans or malicious, they can converse with each other and with people. In real life certain people credit animals with human qualities or talents: in mythology this tendency is greatly magnified.

The dragon is the oldest creature in mythology, but the fox is the oldest in superstition. Apart from these, the dog, the cat and the badger recur most frequently. The fox is used as a messenger by the Rice god, Inari, and indeed the god is sometimes depicted as a fox. Like other animals, the fox is able to transform itself into human

shape, although it does not do this as often as the serpent or dragon. It is generally the serpent which demands human sacrifices, as in the case of the dragon in whose tail Susano found the sword and also of the sea or dragon gods to whose mercies Yamamoto's consort threw herself. Badgers vary in temperament: they can be tricksters, self-transformers, grateful friends or fools, easily bemused by guile. Often the badger is pictured in the garb of a Buddhist monk in which case the animal is symbolising the virtue of gratitude.

The white hare of Oki

The oldest animal story of all, however, other than those concerning serpents or dragons, is about a hare. It appears in the *Kojiki* but not in the *Nihongi*. The chief mortal or rather deity in it is Oh-kuni-nushi, Great Land Master, whose marriage to Susano's daughter has already been described. The setting is again Izumo, and the Island of Oki.

Left: relief of a curled up dragon carved from natural wood. It is believed to have been an ornament in a temple. The eyes are coloured gold, with black pupils. Kamakura period (1185-1333). Museum für Völkerkunde, Vienna.

Right: a seventeenth century wooden carving of a sitting fox. The fox is the messenger of Inari, the God of Rice, and guardian of the rice crop. But the animal is feared too for its malevolence, and to be possessed by a fox spirit is sometimes thought to be a cause of insanity, depression and hysteria. Museum für Völkerkunde, Vienna.

There was a white hare on the island who had a great yearning to visit the Izumo peninsula, the area known as Inaba in particular. It was unable to swim and reached the mainland by trickery. There were crocodiles all around the coast of Oki and the hare contrived an argument with one of them as to whether there were more hares on Oki than crocodiles in the sea. So that the number of crocodiles could be calculated, the hare arranged for them to line up in the water, and by jumping along their backs, counting as it went, it finally reached the Izumo coast. The last crocodile guessed the motive behind the hare's activities and pulled out all its fur as the animal bounded onto the beach.

It was in this denuded condition that a group of brothers, on their way to court the Princess of Inaba, found the hare. They taunted it and suggested that if it washed in sea water and lay in the wind, its hair would grow again. Naturally this treatment was useless, and when

Netsuke illustrating the scene from the story of The Tongue-Cut Sparrow, when the wicked woman opens her box and is chastened and killed by demon creatures. British Museum.

the youngest of the brothers, Oh-kuni-nushi, arrived at the beach the hare was in considerable pain. Oh-kuni-nushi bathed the small animal in fresh water and dusted its skin with pollen – and the white fur grew again. The hare conversed with Oh-kuni-nushi and told him how it had arrived on the peninsula. It learned how its rescuer, although the youngest brother, also wished to woo the Princess of Inaba. They travelled together and found that the Princess had rejected all the other brothers as suitors. She was charmed by Oh-kuni-nushi and with his little companion, and the pair were married. Oh-kuni-nushi became ruler in Izumo and the white hare of Oki made its home with the couple.

The tongue-cut sparrow
Another tale of speech between animals – or, in this case, birds – and men is the famous one of the Tongue-Cut Sparrow. The less familiar version of this is very short. An old woman nursed a sick sparrow to health and then released it. It flew away and then returned, giving her a little seed and telling her to plant it. This she did and it produced an abnormally large crop of gourds filled with delicious pulp. The dried gourds then furnished an inexhaustible store of rice for the kind old woman. Her envious next-door neighbour determined to have such fortune. She struck at a sparrow, stunned it and then looked after it until it had recovered. Again a gift of a single seed was given, but this one produced a poor plant and the pulp of the few gourds it bore was inedible. She dried the remaining fruit, hoping at least to have an endless supply of rice. The few gourds were heavy and she sincerely believed her rice would indeed be self-replenishing. However, the gourds contained bees, scorpions, centipedes and other stinging insects which swarmed on her and stung her to death.

The better known version of this tale is the same in essence. The wicked neighbour, a washer-woman, cut the tongue of a sparrow in punishment for pecking at her rice starch. The bird, which had been fed regularly by the old couple next door, flew away and the kind couple went in search of it. They found it and its family and were offered the choice of two boxes to take away, having been entertained by a feast and dancing display first. The old people chose the smaller of the boxes and when they opened it on their return they found it contained an endless supply of riches: gold, silks and precious stones. The washer-woman set out, motivated by envy, to find the Tongue-Cut Sparrow and his family. She, too, was entertained in the same way and given the choice of two boxes to take away with her. Typically she chose the larger one and on opening it was seized upon by a horde of devils which devoured her.

The grateful dog
Another story tells of a man who made his money by owning silk worms, but it was his wife who looked after them and did all the work of reeling the silk thread from the cocoons. One year the silk worms died and realising there would be no income from silk, the husband turned his wife from the house. She took nothing with her but the sole surviving silk worm, a few mulberry leaves on which to feed it and also the family dog. One day the dog ate the silk worm – out of pure hunger probably, for this animal does not come into the malicious category – but the woman resisted the temptation to kill it in revenge for having eaten her only other companion.

Not long afterwards, the dog appeared to have a wounded nose and the woman, when tending it, noticed a thin thread hanging from one nostril. This thread was pure silk. She wound it on to a reel and then many reels, for the dog continued to produce a great quantity of silk. After these reels had been sold, the dog died.

Men and Animals

She buried the body under a mulberry tree and suddenly, when she had given thanks to Buddha for the dog which had given her a living, a mass of silk worms appeared on the leaves of the tree. They matured with unnatural speed and within a short time the woman was reeling silk of such magnificent quality that she was able to sell it to the imperial court. Her husband, hearing of this, quickly repented of his former sloth and cruelty and she rejoined him. From the spirit of the dog whose life she did not take in anger came the riches on which the couple lived thereafter.

The grateful bee

Not only birds and animals show gratitude: insects display this virtue also. A warrior, defeated in battle, took refuge in a cave. He

Left: a pair of mandarin ducks. Many stories are told about the devotion of these water birds and they are a popular subject for artists. Painting by Kousai. Victoria and Albert Museum.

Right: Shaka Muni, the Japanese way of pronouncing S'akya Muni, the Chinese name for Gautama Buddha. The entry of Shaka Muni into Nirvana with all of creation in mourning is a popular scene in Japanese art. Jizo appears at the top right of this coloured silk kakemono, leading a small group. Museum für Völkerkunde, Vienna.

noticed a bee there, caught in a spider's web, and set it free. As he slept that night, he dreamed of a man dressed in brown telling him that he was the bee which had been freed and that he would therefore help him win his next battle. The man in brown urged the dreamer to fight even if he had only a few followers and, before even planning the campaign, to build a shed filled with containers or vessels. The hero of the story duly built a hut in the forest and, having collected old jars and pots, rallied his scanty retainers who had also been in hiding. Bees from miles around came and lodged in the receptacles prepared for them. When the enemy forces heard the warrior was at large again with his handful of supporters, they attacked his little shelter in the forest. It seems unnecessary to add that the bees rather than the warrior hero of the story won the day: they swarmed on the enemy and stung them into flight.

Mandarin ducks

Many narratives about the animal world take the form of a dream vision or transformation. For example, there is a story of a man who shot at a pair of mandarin ducks, killing the drake. These birds are associated with happy marriages and, for that reason, are seldom hunted. However, this particular man was in need of food. That night he dreamed of a beautiful woman coming into his room, weeping distractedly and accusing him of murdering her husband. She told him to go to the place where he had hunted the previous day in order to learn of his crime, for, said the dream woman, he did not yet know what he had done. This dream was so real to him that he did return to the riverbank, not taking his bow and quiver with him this time. From where he stood, he saw a mandarin duck swimming alone. Instead of turning away it came towards him and, stepping out of the water at his feet and gazing intently at him, suddenly dropped its head and tore open its breast with its beak, thus killing itself. It is said this man subsequently became a celibate priest in remorse.

Another story about a drake concerns the affection between these water birds, but also is a tale of gratitude. The drake was caught and kept in a cage by a rich man, but was looked after by his manservant. The bird moped and would not eat. A serving girl in the household advised the manservant to release it, as it was clearly pining for its mate and would inevitably die in captivity. The owner of the mandarin duck was furious when he found the bird no longer in its cage and, suspecting the servant of having set it free, treated him with indifference verging on cruelty. The maid was much distressed by the abuse her fellow-servant was getting, for which she was partly responsible. Drawn together in this manner, the couple fell in love.

From then on, there was much gossip in the household about their feelings for one another, and eventually the head of the house came to the conclusion that they had both been responsible for depriving him of his pet bird. Those were days without mercy, for he ordered that their joint punishment was to be death by drowning. Just as this sentence – passed without trial, merely on the order of the master of the house – was about to be carried out, two messengers arrived from the provincial governor with the news that capital punishment had been abolished in the province and that all offenders under sentence were to be taken to the governor immediately. The rich man hastily ordered his two servants to be unbound and he put them in charge of the governor's messengers.

It was a long walk to the capital and the servants followed the officials, who did not speak to them at all. Relief at their reprieve, anxiety as to what the future held, and general fatigue made them trail behind increasingly slowly, until they realised the men they were following had vanished from sight and that they were lost.

They spent the night in an old hut and when the lovers finally slept, the messengers appeared to them saying they were the pair of mandarin ducks, the male of which they had enabled to rejoin its mate. On waking, the couple saw a pair of ducks by the entrance of the hut, which bowed their heads in greeting and then flew away together. The servants naturally never returned to their master, but took employment in another district where they married. Their union was as close as that of the birds who had saved them from death in indebtedness for the preservation of their own marriage.

Filial piety

There is no doubt that the religious beliefs of the Japanese have influenced their beliefs about animals. The idea that everything, animate or inanimate, has a *kami* or soul is of Shinto origin. Buddhism did not actively discourage this belief, and one of the great Buddhist virtues is gratitude, whether it be for a service rendered or for a good family upbringing. An example of filial piety occurs in a legend

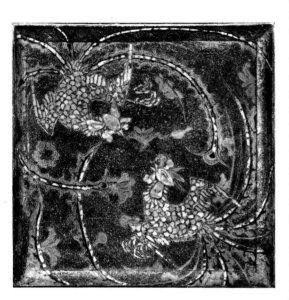

A square tray with upward-turned edges incorporating a phoenix design made of mother of pearl and gold lacquer. Museum für Völkerkunde, Vienna.

Right: a water colour of Jurojin, one of the Seven Gods of Luck. He is frequently shown with a stag, symbolic of old age. Victoria and Albert Museum.

about butterflies. A young man whose work and hobby was gardening married a girl with an identical interest in plant life. They lived only for each other and their shrubs and plants, but in middle age they had a son, who happily inherited his parents' love of flowers.

The parents died within days of one another in old age, when their son was still a youth. The boy looked after his parents' garden and the plants in it more carefully than ever, if that were possible, for he felt they contained the spirits of his dead mother and father. During the first spring following their death he saw each day two butterflies in the garden. Gentle person that he was, he cultivated plants on which he saw the butterflies liked to settle, and as spring turned into summer he dreamed one night that his parents had come back to the garden and were walking round it together, looking at each plant carefully, as gardeners will. Suddenly the couple in the dream turned into butterflies and in this form continued to examine each flower. The next morning the same pair of butterflies were, as usual, in the garden and the boy knew then that the souls of his parents rested in the butterflies and that in that way they still enjoyed their garden.

Ikezuki, the horse

The relationship between man and creatures is not, however, confined purely to the supernatural. Very often heroes have dogs or horses who share their master's prowess: Momotaro, for instance, was accompanied on his exploit by animal retainers, with whom he was able to converse. But the horse Ikezuki, although now a legendary animal, at one time must have been a perfectly normal steed.

Between 1177 and 1181 there used to be an annual horse fair at Asuma. During that period Ikezuki was born. It lost its mother as a young colt and one day, seeing its own reflection in the basin of a waterfall, thought it was its mother and jumped in to join the mare. In this manner Ikezuki taught itself to swim, after several attempts to reach its mother.

The horse's owner put it in charge of a dealer to take it to the fair and on the way they came to a river overflowing its banks from melting snow. On the other side were columns of horses and cattle being taken to the fair and Ikezuki leapt into the rushing water, swam the river and then galloped on alone, ahead of the other animals, to the fair. In due course the horse dealer arrived, but no one would buy the high spirited stallion, for the dealers there were afraid of it, chiefly on account of the curious manner in which it had arrived by itself.

On the way back to the owner the dealer, leading Ikezuki, met a man who looked at the horse and held up six fingers. The dealer thought the man was going to buy the animal for six hundred copper coins and since there was no other chance of selling, he handed Ikezuki over. But in exchange he received six hundred silver coins, and the buyer said that he thought the horse was worth far more. Later Ikezuki was bought by Yoritomo, the victor of the Battle of Dannoura in 1185, when he had set up his shogunate in Kamakura.

Tametomo and his dog

Tametomo has already been mentioned for his part in the struggles against the Tairas in the civil wars of the twelfth century. He was the uncle of Yoshitsune, and is remembered chiefly for his skill with the bow and arrow. There is a charming story of him and his dog, one of the many tales found in every country's folklore of a dog's faithfulness to its master. In his youth Tametomo was sent by his father to a different province to live with another family. Apparently his high spirits were too much for ordinary parental discipline. The boy's dog went with him on the journey, with an accompanying servant. On the way, the man and his charge rested under a pine tree and, in typically Japanese fashion, admired the view. Tametomo's dog suddenly began leaping around him, barking frenziedly. In fury he beheaded it with his sword. But instead of falling, the creature's head flew up into the pine tree where it attacked and killed a dangerous snake. The tree, the dead snake and the head of the dog all crashed to the ground. That Tametomo regretted his outburst goes without saying, and he and the servant buried the head and body of the dog in a carefully dug grave. Tametomo comes out badly from this tale, but his later deeds give history and legend reason to be grateful to the pet of his youth.

Pots for hire

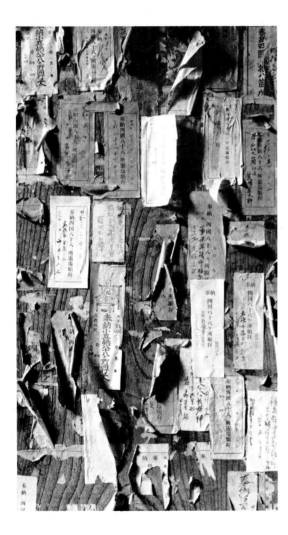

Badgers are often, though not invariably, found to be malicious in folklore. There was a badger called Dankuro which lived in a cave. When a nearby castle had been captured (in a conflict between men, not animals) Dankuro went there and collected a large supply of cooking utensils. This curious form of loot Dankuro would lend to humans, for use at family celebrations. It was made very clear by Dankuro that if the pots and pans were not returned to its cave, it would never lend them out again, which it did without payment or reward. When one of the borrowers did fail to return a bowl, Dankuro not only stopped lending out the goods from the castle, but caused much destruction in the fields around and then set fire to a pile of firewood at the entrance of the cave. Dankuro and the pilfered cooking utensils were never seen again.

Richard M. Dorson in his *Folk Legends of Japan* describes the Dankuro story as a variant of the one about the *kappa* who attacked a horse, trying to pull it down into the pond in which it lived. The horse tried to kick itself free and in doing so the water was spilled from the kappa's head, and its strength was gone. But it clung on and was dragged back to the horse's stables. The owner was furious with the kappa, but forgave it on the understanding that it would lend bowls to him without a fee, whenever he wanted to entertain. So bowls were always to be found in the stable yard the night before a feast was planned and removed again from the yard when they had been used. But a neighbour stole one set of utensils after the owner of the horse had put them outside, having finished with them, and thereafter the kappa never produced any of its sets again on hire or on loan.

The badger and the rabbit

Robert J. Adams, the translator of Keigo Seki's *Folktales of Japan*, states in the headnote to the story Kachi Kachi Mountain that there are some eighty-eight versions of the story in Japan. It includes three common motifs: of the badger being malicious, of humans being able to converse with the animal kingdom and of an animal transformation. A man caught a troublesome badger and, having tied it up, asked his wife to make soup of the animal. The badger pleaded with the woman to let it loose, promising to help her with her cooking. She was beguiled by its entreaties and unbound it, whereupon it killed her, took on her physical appearance, dressed itself in her clothes and proceeded to make soup of *her* carcass. Still in the guise of the man's wife, the badger presented its captor with the soup which the man ate with relish. Only then did the animal turn back into its real form. It mocked the unhappy man for having eaten his own wife and then ran from the house.

A rabbit who had long been friendly with the couple heard of this fearsome trick played on the man and determined to take revenge on the badger. It persuaded the badger to carry a bundle of sticks up a mountain. The rabbit climbed behind and set fire to the bundle.

Men and Animals

The badger heard the sound of burning twigs, but was assured that the sound was that of the Kachi Kachi bird. There is no such bird: the word is onomatopoeic for clicking or snapping. The badger was severely burned, but again was mocked by the rabbit which put a paste of hot pepper on its already painful back, ostensibly to help its healing. The White Hare of Oki was similarly tricked, though not for the sake of vengeance. But the rabbit had still further punishment in store. The gullible badger was persuaded into building a boat of clay. In this it set out to catch fish, while the rabbit accompanied it in a more stoutly constructed craft. As the clay softened and the badger tried to escape from its disintegrating boat, the rabbit struck it with an oar and killed it, leaving its body to float away down the river.

Left: ofudas on a wall at the Muro-ji Temple in Nara. An ofuda is a sticker, sometimes nowadays even just a writing card, left by pilgrims. It usually states how many Buddhist temples the pilgrim has already visited on his journey and how many he intends to visit.

Right: the badger, like the fox, is able to take human form and disguise itself. But it is an amusing rather than a malicious character in tradition and legend. Pottery statues of badgers are quite common and in this photograph two are for sale in a pottery shop. The badgers are depicted in one of their common forms, with a lotus leaf as a hat, carrying a bill for sake (rice wine) and with distended stomachs and scrota. Badgers are reputed to use these parts of their bodies as drums, beating on them with their hands (when in human disguise) or their forepaws.

Malicious cats

The cat can be as malevolent as the badger, as is evidenced by the behaviour of one towards a young boy, although it did not use such refined mental torture. The boy used to hunt daily with a bow and ten arrows only. One day his mother persuaded him to take an extra one, saying he might be in need of it. He shot nothing all day and as the moon rose, he indulged in the very Japanese custom of moon gazing. It is not uncommon for people to give moon-watching parties – to sit and contemplate as the moon rises. As he sat there, he noticed a second moon appear in the sky. He suspected this to be a demonic moon and shot all his arrows at it in swift succession. Ten rebounded, but the last one caused the second moon to emit a fearful screech and there followed a crash in the undergrowth.

The boy, probably from curiosity rather than bravado, ran to the place and found a huge dead cat lying there, with the eleventh arrow in its heart and a large looking-glass between its paws. The boy abandoned his moon gazing and ran home and told his mother of his weird experience. She then informed him she had seen a cat that morning counting the arrows in the quiver and she had feared it would not do this without evil intent. Hence her plea for him to take an extra arrow. With such a foreboding, most mothers surely would have insisted either that the child be accompanied on his hunt or take more than just one extra arrow. However her intuition that one arrow would be enough proved entirely correct.

A whole village was once victimised by a company of supernatural cats. These creatures demanded, and indeed received, the sacrifice of a virgin once a year. Such was the fear of the cats that the villagers annually selected a girl by the drawing of lots. A travelling warrior

heard that this horrible procedure had just taken place for the yearly sacrifice. He begged the parents of the chosen victim to keep close guard on her during the appointed night, and to give him the cage in which the girl to be offered to the cats was always put. Through a dream he knew that the phantom creatures were terrified of someone called Schippeitaro. He made enquiries locally and found that this name actually belonged to a dog. He traced its owner and borrowed the animal.

The dog was then put in the cage and taken to the place in the forest where in previous years a petrified girl had been left to her fate. A group of unearthly cats, led by one larger and more fearsome in appearance than the rest, appeared and danced around the cage. After much jeering and screeching the large cat flung open the door of the cage. Schippeitaro leapt out and seized the cat by its throat. The warrior then decapitated the cat as the others ran wailing away.

Typical farmland in Kyushu. The brilliant yellow rape seed fields are ready for harvest.

Netsuke of Gama-Sennin, the Sage with a Toad. This character, named Kosensei, is generally portrayed with a toad, although he is not always holding it in his hand. There are various tales about Kosensei but they all concern a toad, long life or his ability to turn himself into the form of the reptile. In one version another man turned into a frog in order to watch Kosensei secretly. The sage is said to have been completely hairless with warts or lumps on his skin, both toad-like features. British Museum.

Right: a stone carved frog at the Okitama Shrine at Futami. On clear days it is possible to see Mt Fuji from the beach.

Peasants roistering around a hayrick. In the background foxes can be seen turning into young women. Print by Kuniyoshi. Victoria and Albert Museum.

The badger and the fox cub

Many animal stories involve humans only incidentally. A badger and a vixen with its cub lived near each other and were, supposedly, friends. They had been deprived of prey by human hunters in the forest and in their desperate need for food it was agreed that the fox should change itself into a man, sell the badger (which would pretend to be dead), and with the money received for it buy food and return to the forest, by which time the badger would have run back itself.

The vixen duly took on the form of a man (like the badger of the Kachi Kachi Mountain, it could take on the appearance of the opposite sex when changing into a member of the human race) and the plan worked satisfactorily. The badger then suggested the order

should be reversed. However, when it was in human form, it told the merchant to whom it had sold the vixen – then acting the part of lifelessness – that the animal was not in fact dead at all. So the merchant killed the vixen and the badger-man made some purchases and went back to the forest in its normal shape. It told the cub its mother was dead and did not even allow the little creature to share the food it had brought back.

The cub accordingly took revenge. It suggested a competition whereby they should again take it in turns to appear in human form and whoever guessed the real identity of the other would win. The badger, susceptible to flattery and gullible as badgers so often are, fell in with this plan and allowed the cub to perform its transformation first. But the young fox did no such thing: it hid behind a tree near the road leading to the village. The badger had followed it and when a procession led by the local provincial governor came by, it sprang into the road, shouting out that it had guessed the governor was the cub. This was startling behaviour indeed and in a trice the retainers in the procession killed the badger – to the entertainment and delight of the fox cub watching.

So effectively can animals assume the semblance and manners of men and women that there are a number of stories of marriages between human beings and animals. One tale of such a marriage centres upon a crane. A young man rescued the wounded bird, who in thankfulness turned into a woman and became his dutiful, loved and loving wife. She made beautiful silk brocade which he sold, but one day, against her wishes, he looked into the room where she did her work and saw her in crane form. (He had not appreciated before that his wife was in fact the crane whose life he had saved.)

She was, therefore, bound to fly away and leave him – as happened when the Sea King's daughter had been seen by Fire Fade in her dragon shape while giving birth to the child who was to become the father of the first emperor of Japan.

An example of a creature taking on the form of a tree dates from the eleventh century. It concerns another fox. A man and his servant were searching for a lost horse. They thought they had gone further than they had realised for they came upon a vast cryptomeria, which neither of them recognised. However, the meadow in which it grew was familiar and so were the surrounding landmarks. The tree simply had not been there before.

The two men decided that its sudden growth was the result of some evil at work and they acted as did the boy who saw the second moon; they shot arrows at it. There were no unearthly sounds on this occasion, but the tree vanished. The man and his servant ran home at speed. The following day they ventured out to the same place, but all they found was an old dead fox, with cryptomeria twigs in its mouth. One wonders about the fate of the lost horse in this story: it is not revealed. Nor does one know why the fox elected to change into a tree, unless it was to hinder the search for the horse.

The badger-kettle

There is a tale relating sometimes to a fox but more generally to a badger which turned itself into a tea-kettle. It did this to repay the woodman who had saved its life, and the woodman sold the kettle to a priest. The kettle did not like life in the temple, where it was not only polished (a painful experience apparently) but used on the fire. So it returned to the woodman, in whose debt it was, having thoroughly frightened the acolytes in the temple by moving about and crying out in pain. It continued to make money for the man to whom it had given itself, this time by dancing. The woodman (on occasions he is described as a tinker) became a travelling entertainer, the dancing badger-kettle doing the entertaining.

In another rendering of this story the badger, disliking being used as a kettle in the temple, turned itself into a prostitute. It

Right: netsuke depicting the old man who made the cherry trees bloom. He is shown about to scatter the ashes which bring the trees into full blossom. British Museum.

Far right: the three monkeys over one of the gates at the mausoleum of the first Tokugawa shogun, Ieyasu, at Nikko. The complex of buildings is known as the Toshogu (Ieyasu's posthumous name) Shrine. The monkeys are known as Koshin and are supposed neither to hear, speak or hear evil. They are often portrayed in relief in stone, but this wooden carving is probably the most famous of Koshin in Japan.

made money for its new owner to whom the woodman sold it (saying the 'badger' was his daughter) for a large sum. But the badger finally tired of this occupation and became a horse and again its rescuer sold it for a considerable amount of money. However, the badger died of its labours in horse form, for while it was able to transform its shape, it was unable to give itself the strength of a horse.

In the versions of the story where the transformations into prostitute and horse are omitted, the badger-kettle either tells its owner it is going to die, in which case it is presented in kettle form to the temple and not used but revered, or it is given back to the priest owner, with instructions not to use or polish it and then it lives happily, if lazily, ever after.

As has been shown in the stories of the Kachi Kachi Mountain and of the badger, the vixen and the cub, animals play tricks on each other. They do this whether there are mortals involved or not. In the following illustration deities are concerned, but to a comparatively minor degree.

How the jelly-fish lost its bones

It is sometimes said to be the bride of the Dragon King and sometimes a daughter of his who had a craving for the liver from a live monkey. In one rendering a priest of the Dragon Kingdom under the sea advised her to eat such food in order to cure an illness. Cravings for certain foods are, of course, known to accompany some pregnancies and one may surmise that the dragon deity was pregnant. The tale is set at the time when jelly-fish had bones, fins, a tail and even feet. One of these creatures was dispatched to dry land to fetch a monkey.

A victim was quickly found by the shore and it accepted an invitation to see the wonders of the kingdom beneath the waves. However, on the way to the palace of the Dragon King the jelly-fish related to the monkey the purpose of the invitation. The monkey replied that as its liver was so heavy, it generally took it out during the day time and that it must go and fetch it from the tree where it had been left. So the jelly-fish took the monkey back to the place where they had met. Pointing to a tree, the monkey said it thought its liver had been stolen, but that it would go and look for its missing organ, and in the meantime the jelly-fish should go back to the sea and explain what had happened.

When the Dragon King heard the explanation he beat the jelly-fish into the shape these creatures now have, and the craving for a live monkey's liver either disappeared or the female dragon

deity recovered from her illness without its aid. This story is also told with an octopus taking the part of the jelly-fish, similarly having its bones removed in punishment for having been taken in by the monkey's wit.

Enmity between monkeys and crabs

In the next story – and there are numerous renderings of it – the monkey does not fare so well. It exchanged with a crab a piece of rice cake for a persimmon seed. In an unnaturally short time the seed grew into a tree covered with fruit, and the crab perfectly reasonably asked the monkey to pick the persimmons as it was unable to do so itself. The monkey ate the ripe fruit and threw the unripe persimmons at the crab, which at once retaliated by calling out a string of obscenities at the monkey. The monkey in resentment then defecated into the crab's burrow. Reprisal was easy for the crab: it seized the monkey's buttocks with its pincers and did not release its grip until the animal gave it some of its hairs. This was a strange request from a crab, but it is said to explain why certain species of crab have hairs on their pincers.

In another version, while the beginning of the story is substantially the same, the crab retaliates violently, not because of the monkey's act at the entrance to its home, but because of the indignity of having its own persimmons thrown at it. It enlists the aid of various objects and also that of a bee. The monkey is invited to the crab's house and is then badly burned by an exploding egg in the fire, stung in the face by the bee, made to fall by stepping on seaweed strategically placed, and then crushed by a falling mortar and pestle. In another version, war had been declared between all monkeys and all crabs, and the visitor to the crab's home was the Monkey King who came alone to discuss treaty terms. The various tortures

A household altar. Various deities are shown on a cliff face, with water below. At the foot of the slope there is an entrance to a cave made of polychromed wood. Benten, with eight arms, is in the centre, with a Shinto torii in her crown. Bishamon is on her right and Daikoku on her left. The rest of the figures are worshippers in peasant clothes carrying various tools and utensils. Museum für Völkerkunde, Vienna.

were inflicted on it and finally the crab army pinched it to death.

The laws of nature do not include kindness in the animal world. This is very apparent in animal legend, with its stress on vengeance and trickery. But the affection which exists between so many men and their dogs seems to be world-wide: it certainly does appear in the dog and master stories of Japan. Supernatural marriages between mortals and serpents and animals and birds may have some connection with the warmth with which some men and women down the ages have regarded animals and particularly their pets.

If the Buddhists brought gratitude as a virtue to Japan, it is a human characteristic which those who enjoy the company of animals are inclined to attach to the non-human. So it is surely not surprising that as the old stories of men and animals have been embroidered down the years, the threads of gratitude and loyalty have been used constantly in the stitching.

*Urashima Taro and the daughter of the
Dragon King.*

Urashima

Basil Hall Chamberlain, who put the *Kojiki* into English (and Latin
where he thought it advisable), translated the story of Urashima
from a classical Japanese poem, and W.G. Aston, the translator of
the *Nihongi* (who also used Latin in a few instances), wrote a
prose version. Since then it has been constantly retold.

Urashima was a young man and worked as a fisherman. He saved
a tortoise (although some believe it was a turtle) from death on
the beach where it had been turned on its back by some louts. In
other renderings he caught the tortoise while fishing and let it go
free. The point is that the tortoise is one of the symbols of old age
and to be respected as such.

Later, when out in his boat, Urashima saw the creature again
and they spoke together. The water creature revealed itself to be
the daughter of the Dragon King of the Sea and transformed itself

into a young woman of great beauty. Urashima accompanied her to the kingdom under the sea. There they fell in love and were married, with the full approval of the Dragon King. After a while Urashima hankered to see his homeland again and to visit his parents, for he wished to tell them of his marriage and to ensure they were well cared for in their advancing years. His bride was unhappy about this, but she accepted the situation when Urashima promised to return to her. It was not a difficult promise to make: he wanted his marriage to continue. She gave him a box and extracted another promise from him to the effect that he would not open it while on his visit. It was a lacquer box, fastened with a silk cord, and Urashima's wife said that if he did open it, he would not see her again.

In her tortoise shape she escorted him back to the shore and

then left him on dry land to make his own way to his old home. When he arrived he was dismayed to find that all seemed changed. The contours of the surrounding hills were the same, but the village looked different and he could not find his parents' house. The villagers too were all strangers to Urashima. He asked without avail as to his parents' whereabouts until he met an old, old man who said they had been dead for centuries and that their only son, named Urashima, had been drowned at sea four hundred years before.

In dismay the youth returned to the beach, realising that his time in the kingdom of the sea had not been measured by mortal years. Perhaps to find an answer to the riddle of time, perhaps out of forgetful curiosity as to the contents of the parting gift his wife had given him, he broke his promise to her and opened the box. The years, in the form of a thin wisp of smoke, wafted out of it.

His hair turned grey, then white. His body contracted and his face became lined. His eyes dimmed and then his heart stopped its work. The centuries had caught up with Urashima and the villagers later found the body of a very aged man lying on the sand. Hearn quotes the date of Urashima's last fishing expedition as A.D. 477 and that of his return and death as A.D. 825. In the *Nihongi*, the date of his departure is given as A.D. 478. In a myth of this antiquity a difference of one year is no difference at all: for all its retellings, the story remains basically the same.

The woodcutter and the Fountain of Youth
Time, coupled with a marriage, are again the themes in a tale of a

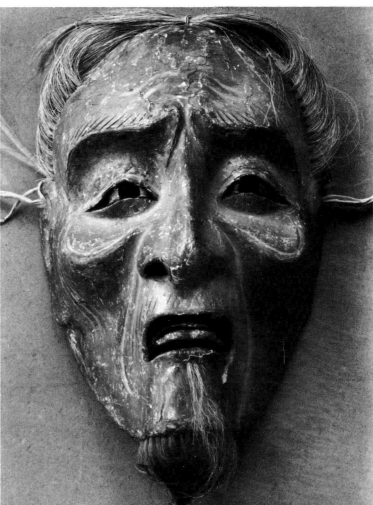

Left: the inside of the lid of a gold lacquer box, nearly a foot in length. Urashima Taro is about to open the box which cost him his life at a great and unnatural age. The pine trees and the storks are symbolic of old age. Twelfth-century treasure box. Seattle Art Museum.

Right: a Noh mask.

woodcutter. This man was old at the outset of the story. On a hot day he became thirsty and drank from a stream from which, for no particular reason, he had never drunk before. The water was clear and flowed swiftly and had a peculiarly delicious taste.

The stream came from a small pool and he went to it, the better to quench his thirst. As he knelt down he saw his reflection in the pool and it was all but unrecognisable: he saw the face which had been his as a young man. Joyously he realised he had drunk from the Fountain of Youth. Running in a manner of which he had not been capable for many years, he returned home to his wife. After some difficulty he persuaded her that he who spoke with the voice she knew well and whose features, for all their youthfulness, were familiar, was indeed her husband.

*A six-fold screen depicting a cherry tree in full
blossom. Groves of cherry trees are found
throughout Japan, and many stories are connected
with cherry blossom. The crest of the imperial army
was a single cherry blossom. Musée Guimet, Paris.*

Reasonably she said she, too, must drink of the same water: he would soon tire of a wife so many years older than he had become. The woodcutter told her where the little pool from which the stream sprang was and, alone, she hurried on her way. Her husband waited for her with considerable impatience and, doubtless, curiosity. When, after an interval during which she should have returned, there was no sign of her, he went in search of his wife who was, like him, to be young again.

He reached the pool and there, lying on the bank, was a baby girl. The old woman in her eagerness had drunk too much of the Fountain of Youth. The story ends there, and it is hard not to speculate on the future of the marriage of the woodcutter and his wife who had tampered with time.

Gingko trees

If there were an end to that story, perhaps the kami of the gingko (maidenhair) tree would come into it, for the gingko's spirit is said to care for nursing mothers and tend their supply of milk. Or perhaps the woodcutter fed his infant wife with *midzu-ame* as did the ghost of the woman whose baby was born after her death. There is a legend of an old gingko tree in a park in Tokyo which was dying for no apparent reason. An old woman appeared to one of the gardeners there and told him that, as it was the milk tree, only milk would revive it. Cow's milk was poured round its trunk and the tree did revive.

The short-lived dynasty of shoguns, which Yoritomo founded, came to an end in 1219 under a gingko tree, now said to be over a thousand years old, in the grounds of the Hachiman temple in Kamakura. Yoritomo's second son, Sanetomo, was shogun. He was preparing to go in procession to the temple and had a foreboding that all was not well. He pulled a single hair from his head and gave it to a servant, telling him to keep it in memory of him. In spite of the warnings he was then given, Sanetomo did not put on armour under his ceremonial robes. When the cavalcade reached the gingko tree the high priest (who was Sanetomo's nephew) sprang out from behind it and decapitated him. The nephew was caught and executed, but strangely enough the shogun's head was not found. The servant produced the hair his master had given him and this was buried in place of the head. The gingko tree marks the spot where the Minamoto shogunate came to an end and the beginning of the era of the Hojo regents.

Gingko trees, in addition to their association with milk, are reputed to be the only members of the vegetable world which possess the human quality of loyalty: it is said they will die on occasion for their masters. Certainly in Shimo Niban Cho, Kojimachi-ku in Tokyo, when fire raged through the area following the Great Earthquake of 1 September 1923, the only house which was saved had a gingko tree growing over it. Apparently the intense heat caused the tree to exude moisture: it died in the preservation of the house in the garden of which it grew. The plum tree which followed Tenjin into exile must also have had the attribute of loyalty, unless it was its master's love for the tree which caused it to fly across the sea.

The old man and the cherry tree

There is an ancient tale of an old man who loved cherry trees and was given the power of being able to make them bloom. It is a combination of a plant story and an animal story. The old man had a wife and together they cared for their dog. They were poor and their only form of entertainment was exercising the animal and looking at the cherry blossom in the spring. One year the couple took their dog walking to see a particularly fine display of blossom.

127

Right: the Kasuga Shrine at Nara was founded in 768 by the Fujiwara family. There are a great number of lanterns in the extensive grounds.

A stone image of Jizo. Rijksmuseum voor Volkenkunde, Leiden.

On the way home the dog scratched in the ground, and in the hole it made they found a heap of golden coins. Their poverty was thus ended. An evil neighbour, not unlike the one in the story of the Tongue-Cut Sparrow, was consumed with jealousy. He borrowed the dog, forced it to dig a hole and when only waste matter was found, killed it.

The kind old couple buried the animal under a flowering cherry in their garden. They considered the dog's kami lived in the tree and for that reason were loth to lop one of the branches, even when it threatened the house. However, in the end they did so and from the wood fashioned a mortar, feeling that in that way the kami would at least be useful.

There was a famine that year, and in spite of their new wealth they had little rice to pound. When the wife used the mortar for the first time, she found the flour filled the mortar to overflowing. Through the cherry wood mortar and the dog's spirit, they were provided with a never-ending supply of food. As they had shared their wealth with those less fortunate than themselves in the village, so they distributed flour for the duration of the famine. The evil neighbour was not content with this and begged for the loan of the mortar. In generous but foolish fashion they lent it to him. But for him no flour came – just a mass of stinging insects and crawling creatures. In fury he burned the mortar.

He did, however, allow the old man to collect the ashes and these the man threw on the dog's grave under the cherry tree. Although it was long before cherry blossom time, the tree immediately came into bloom. The old man spent the remainder of his days making the trees bloom in and out of season, using the pieces of ash from the mortar.

Of the host of legends about cherry trees there is one which concerns a wet-nurse named O-Sode. She was engaged to feed a baby girl, the only child of parents not in their first youth. At the age of fifteen this child became seriously ill and O-Sode, who loved her dearly, went and prayed at the temple daily for three weeks for her recovery. At the end of that time the sickness left the girl and she was pronounced fully cured.

The parents gave a party to celebrate their child's escape from death and during the celebrations O-Sode was suddenly taken ill. The next morning her condition had worsened and she told the girl's parents that she had in fact prayed that the fatal illness should be transferred to her and that she would die that day in place of their daughter. Her last request, for she did indeed die, was that a cherry tree should be planted in the garden of the temple where her supplications had been answered. This dying wish was honoured and the tree always bloomed on the anniversary of O-Sode's death, allegedly for over a hundred and fifty years. It was called The Cherry Tree of the Milk Nurse, not only because of O-Sade's work but because the flowers looked like nipples splashed with milk.

The use of the cucumber has already been referred to as a palliative against the evil intent of the kappa. The vegetable occurs in a number of tales with a completely different connotation. One family, who use a design of a cross-section of a cucumber as their crest, claim that the kami of the cucumber centuries ago took the family under its protection after their ancestors had made a vow never to eat cucumbers. And there is a tale of a doctor who had to make a rapid escape from his home village as he had been discovered to be guilty of an offence, presumably connected with his profession. In his hurry he tripped over the curling main stalk of a cucumber plant, lost ground and was captured and killed. His was a violent death and his spirit became a vengeful ghost, taking the form of a small insect known as a *shiwan* which feeds on cucumbers.

Although no mention of an association with kappa comes in this story, it is strange that those creatures, too, are often affiliated with people and things medical.

A Taira ghost

There is a strange tale of a man called Ito who, six hundred years after a Taira warrior, Shigehira, had been executed at the hands of Yoritomo in Kamakura, was guided to a lonely house in the woods. There he was introduced and even wedded to a beautiful girl, who he was told was Shigehira's daughter. Ito realised he was surrounded by apparitions, but their presence was very real to him and he did not find it disturbing. Indeed, during the one night he spent in the ghostly mansion, he became greatly attracted by the charms of his

new and phantom wife. Before they parted she told him they would meet again in ten years time, and that all the Taira clan would rejoice to see him as her bridegroom. For ten years Ito told no one of his experience and during that period he became ill and feeble.

When the time came for their reunion, to which for all his frailty Ito looked forward with eagerness, the ghostly servant girl who had first guided him to the house of Shigehira's daughter appeared to Ito and said his wife was about to summon him. By then he was a very sick man. He told his mother the story for the first time, showing her a gift his bride had given him a decade before, and then he died. Perhaps he did indeed see his wife again.

A legend concerning trees and a tengu springs from a hero much further back in time than the Tairas and the Minamotos. Yamamoto Date, mythological warrior and an emperor's son and an emperor's father, is reputed to have once hung his hat on a pine tree. A fiery object is said to have been seen moving between this tree and a cedar growing near a shrine some little distance away. The object was a tengu which had two homes, one at the top of each tree, and regularly travelled from one dwelling to the other. The creature appeared to do no harm or mischief: it was just there.

The woodcutters' wens

A well known story concerns two woodcutters with lumps, or wens, on their faces. In some versions they met devils or oni on the mountain. In other versions the creatures are tengu and these seem more likely in the circumstances. Each of the woodcutters had a wen on his cheek: one on the left cheek and the other on the right. The man with the disfigured left cheek was a churlish fellow, suspicious, jealous and with few friends. He also happened to be a bachelor, though this hardly affects the story. The other woodcutter was different in that he was cheerful, friendly and married. That neither of them had pride in their wens goes without saying, but one was resigned to what he believed to be an unjust stroke of fate and the other accepted the fact with patience and even gaiety. One evening the pleasant woodcutter was delayed from returning home down the mountain when his work was done by a violent thunder storm. He took shelter in a hollow tree at the edge of a glade.

When the rain stopped and the storm moved away down the valley, he saw to his astonishment a troop of weird creatures filing into the glade in front of him. They formed a circle and began to dance, using steps and contortions which he had never seen before. He remained hidden in the tree trunk until he was infected by the chanting and singing of the dancers and came out to join them. They were a merry company for all their strange appearance and encouraged their new companion to dance a solo. This he did to their great satisfaction. Indeed, so pleased were they by his performance that they begged him to return the following night and dance for them again. It would seem they were unaware that the woodcutter regarded the wen on his cheek as a deformity, for it intrigued them and the one who appeared to be their leader suddenly snatched it from him, saying they would keep it as a forfeit against his return. The wrenching of the lump from his face was utterly painless and the woodcutter was delighted to find he had a smooth cheek to match the other. He hurried home, since the storm had entirely abated by this time, and his wife rejoiced with him over his new facial appearance.

It so happened that the woodcutter with a wen on his left cheek called on the couple that night in order to borrow some household implement. Naturally he was curious about the disappearance of his neighbour's wen – jealous too – and he was told the story. He persuaded the good-natured man to let him take his place and dance for the creatures the following evening, and listened carefully as to how to reach the forest glade up the mountain.

The next evening he hid in the hollow tree trunk and as darkness fell was much afraid as the group of unearthly beings assembled for their dance. His impatience to be rid of his wen overcame his fear and he burst into their midst and began to dance himself. He was not so skilled a performer as his neighbour, or perhaps his dance was a joyless thing. Whatever the reason, the company were displeased with the show he put on and called him, quite rightly, an imposter. This did not deter him and he went on with his cavorting until the creatures forced him to stop. Then their leader mocked him for his incompetence and bewailed the non-arrival of the woodcutter who danced so well and whose forfeit he had.

As it would seem the creature had admired the other woodcutter's wen the motive for its next action is obscure: pure disappointment, perhaps. It drew the wen from beneath its garments and slapped it on the woodcutter's right cheek and then, calling to its followers, led them, dancing and singing the while, across the glade into the dark forest. The wen which had grown on the cheek of his neighbour was immovable and the woodcutter went through the rest of his life with two wens instead of one. Whether his nature changed as well as his facial appearance and whether it changed for better or worse is a matter for conjecture.

Benten, bringer of happiness

Benten, the only female among the gods of Luck, has numerous accomplishments ascribed to her in addition to her elevated position

Left: Benten in her eight-armed incarnation sitting on a lotus throne above the sea. Kakemono. Museum für Völkerkunde, Vienna.

Right: central altar at Kuwayama Shrine, Kyoto. The white horse receives confessions, which because of his big ears he can hear even when made in a whisper.

as goddess of the Sea. Literature and music come under her patronage, but she is regarded also as a giver of wealth and romantic happiness. The worship of Benten has increased in popularity since the twelfth century, possibly because of Kiyomori's meeting with her at sea. Indeed, the sea appears to be her home and she is thought to be the daughter of the Dragon King, in his human-like form, wearing a crown with a serpent on it. Tawara Toda's encounter with the Dragon King, the story which includes the King's daughter, is surely associated with Benten: the daughter did not marry the human hero and great were the benefits he received after killing the giant centipede. Benten is also associated with Lake Biwa, the locale of that story.

Kyoto and Kamakura, particularly the island of Enoshima just off the coast near Yoritomo's capital, are also associated with her. There is a shrine to her on the island (or peninsula, depending on the

tide). The association of Benten with dragons and the sea seems
to culminate in Enoshima, and the fact that she is depicted either
riding or being escorted by a dragon so frequently would appear to be
because of the Enoshima story rather than on account of her father.
There is a tale that before Enoshima appeared, a dragon lived on the
mainland near the strip of sand which now connects it at low tide to
the island. This dragon used to eat children in the village now known
as Koshigoe, very near Enoshima and Kamakura. It was in this
same village that Nichiren escaped decapitation through a miracle in
the thirteenth century. In the sixth century an earthquake caused
Enoshima to erupt, with Benten appearing in the sky above it. She
then stepped onto the island and married the dragon. This caused the
dragon's appetite for human flesh to cease. In another version she
married one of the dragon kings after his constant wooing: he was
exceedingly ugly and had the form of a serpent. The cave on Enoshima
is also reputed to have been the home of the dragon or serpent
husband of Benten, and it is said further that there is an underground
tunnel running from the cave to the base of Mount Fuji.

Benten's pictures and images sometimes show her with eight arms,
two of which are folded in prayer, and in that form she resembles
Kwannon, the goddess of Mercy. Their images are occasionally
together in temples and their representation of kindness is
undoubtedly similar. Benten traditionally used a white serpent as her
messenger, but she used another in the legend about her which is
based in Kyoto.

It was in 1701, according to Lafcadio Hearn, just before the Forty-
Seven Ronin embarked on their enterprise, that Benten acted as
go-between in a strange and romantic tale in Kyoto. In the grounds
of the Amadera Temple, a young educated man named Baishu
noticed a newly constructed pool near a spring at which he had
been accustomed to drink. He also noticed for the first time a tablet
near it inscribed 'Birth-Water' and an equally new temple dedicated
to Benten. As he wondered about these, a scrap of paper fluttered
through the air and settled at his feet. On it, in beautiful calligraphy
inscribed by a young female hand, was a love poem with which he
was familiar.

He took the paper home and studied it carefully. The writing was
exquisite and from it he deduced the writer to be both delightful and
accomplished. He resolved to discover her identity and to marry her.
As the paper had come to him while at the Benten-of-the-Birth-Water
Temple in the grounds of Amadera Temple, he returned there to
seek Benten's aid. He was not the first to pray to her for a happy
marriage, and by no means the last.

At the temple he vowed to pray there daily for a week and to
spend the night of the seventh day in vigil. Shortly before dawn as
his night of prayer was ending, he heard someone seeking admittance
into the main temple grounds, and then footsteps approaching the
little temple dedicated to Benten. An old man, venerable in
appearance, joined him in there and immediately afterwards a
beautifully dressed and handsome young man appeared from behind
the screen of the inner sanctuary. The young man spoke to the old
one, saying that his help was sought to bring about a union for which
prayers had been said devotedly. Without a word the old man took
a red cord from his sleeve and tied one end around the wondering
Baishu. The other end he put into the flame of one of the temple
lanterns, and when it was burning, circled it in the air. He had
barely finished doing this when a young woman came into the
Benten-of-the-Birth-Water Temple and sat beside Baishu. She kept
her fan up to her face, but he could see she was very beautiful.
The handsome young man spoke then to Baishu directly for the
first time. He told him his prayers had been heeded by Benten and

that she had caused him to summon the old man to bring about the union. He said further that the young woman who had joined them was the writer of the poem he had found. Then the two men and the woman all vanished, Baishu was alone – and it was daylight. These angelic beings whom Benten had used for her purpose were certainly not serpents or even part of the kingdom of the sea.

As he walked home, Baishu met a girl he instantly recognised as the apparition who had joined him in the temple. He addressed her, but made no mention of having seen her before. She was evidently quite unconcerned at being spoken to by an apparent stranger and answered perfectly naturally. They walked slowly towards Baishu's house together, neither mentioning their meeting in the temple. Indeed, the young woman appeared to be unaware of its having happened, while Baishu's mind and emotions must have been reeling after the events of his night of vigil.

As they reached the gate she suddenly announced that Benten had already made her his wife. Baishu did not need to persuade her to come into his home with him. For some months they lived there together as man and wife. None of their neighbours took any notice of Baishu's changed circumstances: it was as though the young woman was invisible to all but her husband, and to him she was real indeed. Their satisfaction together was total and she delighted him further with her intelligence and artistic accomplishments. He was a cultured man and they were well matched.

As the autumn turned to winter, Baishu was wandering alone through an area of Kyoto he did not know well. A servant came up to him and asked him to accompany him and wait upon his master. Baishu knew neither the servant nor his employer, but he went. To Baishu's astonishment, the servant's master told him that he knew him as his future son-in-law. He explained that, anxious to arrange a suitable marriage for his only daughter, he had scattered poems which she had copied down by all the temples in Kyoto dedicated to Benten, having previously prayed to the goddess for help. Benten then appeared to him in a dream, saying that a good husband had been found for his daughter and that he would meet him during the coming winter. The previous night Benten had again come to him while he slept and said that the future husband of his daughter would pass near his house the following day and that it would be in order to send for him. She gave the girl's father a minute description of his future son-in-law's appearance, and it corresponded exactly with that of Baishu. Before Baishu could explain that he was already married, the man slid open the door leading into the next room, and there was the waiting bride, no other than the young woman Benten had already made his wife in the temple.

They had an earthly wedding and in their marriage were as well suited as they had been before it. It would seem that after the marriage arranged by her father, the girl never referred to her previous time with Baishu, for then it had been her soul with whom Baishu had lived, her soul in bodily form. In the second marriage the union was truly complete, for he was then with her soul and body. Doubtless Benten wished to test Baishu as a husband before giving the young woman to him completely. The question of how she behaved in her father's house while her soul was married to Baishu cannot be answered.

Often the spirit or soul of a lover comes to its partner after death. In the story of Baishu the order was unusually reversed for the girl's spirit came before she was married.

The white butterfly
There is a tale of romantic love which has nothing to do with Benten but which concerns a dead soul appearing as a butterfly. This is

Left: another representation of Benten. She is playing a biwa, the musical instrument of which she is reputed to be so fond. Ink and colour wash painting by Yoshinobu, late eighteenth century. Museum für Völkerkunde, Vienna.

The lid of an iron box, the embossed design depicting a mask. By Myochin Munchisa, about 1525. Museum für Völkerkunde, Vienna.

The Sea Wife carrying away one of the Jewels of the Sea from the Dragon King's palace, chased by his retainers. Print by Kuniyoshi. Victoria and Albert Museum.

a usual form in Japanese lore. Unless Buddhist vows of celibacy are taken it is uncommon, in a country where arranged marriage is accepted, for a man to end his days a bachelor. There was such a man who died in his seventies. He had lived alone for years and was a recluse, but as the illness which proved to be his last one worsened he invited the widow of his only brother and her son, his nephew, to come to him. He was fond of them both, though he saw them seldom.

One day, while sitting with his uncle, the young man saw an enormous white butterfly come into the room. It fluttered, then perched upon the old man's pillow. The nephew tried to brush it away but it persisted. Fearing it would make the sick man restless, he went on trying to make it fly out of the house. Then the youth

wondered whether it might not be an evil spirit, so unnatural was its behaviour, circling his uncle's bedding. At this point the butterfly suddenly, of its own accord, flew straight out of the window. The boy's suspicions were thoroughly aroused and he followed it. His patient was asleep and could be left with safety.

The white butterfly flew swiftly straight to the local cemetery, which was just across the road from the house. It went directly to a tomb and then vanished. As it had disappeared, the nephew returned to the house, having noticed that the old but fairly recently tended grave where the butterfly had vanished was inscribed with the name Akiko.

He had been away only a few minutes, but during that interval his uncle had died. Later when he described to his mother the visit of the butterfly just before his uncle's death and his chase of the insect, she told him that as a young man her brother-in-law and a girl named Akiko had been deeply in love, but Akiko had died just before the day arranged for their marriage. He had bought a house near her grave, looked after the tomb carefully for over fifty years, and never spoken of his half century of mourning to anyone. His sister-in-law knew well the cause of his self-imposed seclusion and respected it: she herself had been a young and happy bride at the time of Akiko's betrothal and subsequent death. The woman had no doubt at all that it was Akiko's spirit in the form of a white butterfly which had come to fetch the spirit of the man she loved at the close of his mortal life.

The unusual dowry

A tale involving mother-love concerns a wooden bowl. The father was already dead when the mother fell mortally ill. She gave to the only child of the marriage, a daughter, a wooden bowl. This is generally described as being lacquered plain black. She instructed the girl to put it on her head. She also told her it would never be possible to take it off: the time would come when the bowl would come off of its own accord. With this as her only legacy the girl had a miserable life, carrying the curiously heavy and immovable bowl on her head. Eventually she got employment in the kitchen of a farming family. The son, home for a visit after a long period of work in Kyoto, caught sight of her and, in spite of the bowl, fell in love with her. He begged her parents to allow him to marry her. After a time they gave their permission, but with reluctance; the girl had nothing as a dowry, and anyway, there was the bowl.

The girl herself was unhappy about the marriage for the same reasons as her future in-laws, but she loved their son and finally gave in to his entreaties. After the exchange of three cups of sake, the central point in the wedding ceremony, the bowl suddenly split into many parts, and there cascaded into the bride's lap a large quantity of gold and silver coins and precious stones. Her dead mother had ensured the girl would have not only an unselfish and good husband but a fortune to take with her into her new home.

Marriage is a constantly recurring theme. It is central in the story of the mouse wedding. The parents of the girl mouse tried to betroth her to Rice, Water, the Sun, the Wind and Thunder as well as other such beings or elements. The mice aimed high, but all those they approached refused, telling the parents of the young mouse of another who was mightier and who would thus be more suitable as a son-in-law. Rice, for instance, said that Water was mightier, for without it it could not grow. In the end, the mouse was married to another mouse. Again animals are depicted with human traits, able to speak with those not of their own kind, but what is peculiarly Japanese is the stress laid upon the arranged marriage between those of equal rank.

And the heroic theme is endless, too. Even in the comparatively modern historical story of the Forty-Seven Ronin a man who had insulted Kuranosuke during the period when the ronin were living incognito and planning their assault on Kira Kozuke-no-Suke's mansion, committed hara-kiri himself in penitence after the ronin had carried out their plans. He did it in front of Kuranosuke's grave, to ensure his spirit would be aware of the self-inflicted punishment, and he is buried with the company of ronin. His grave makes the forty-ninth, for the forty-seven were buried with their daimyo master, Asano.

There are two tales which appear not to have been written in English before. One is clearly Buddhist in origin but would appear to be indigenous to Japan. A man had an unlovable mother: she was mean and bad tempered. He died after her and when he reached heaven, he found his mother was not there but in hell. He was, perhaps, fond of her: he certainly felt he had a duty towards her. So he asked Buddha if she might come up and join him. The reply

was that if the man could find one single kind act which his mother
had done in her life, she could come. After considerable investigation
one kindly action was discovered. The woman had once given a leek
to a beggar who had come to her house. That was her only known show
of charity during her earthly life. So the leek was produced and lowered
down to her. She was told to clutch it and by it she would be lifted
up to heaven. Anxiously her son watched the operation. But it was to
no avail. The leek would not bear her weight and broke. The vegetable
she had given the beggar was a rotten one, which was why she had
let him have it, and why it could not lift her up to heaven. Meanness
was her very nature.

The other tale not previously retold in English comes from the
northern part of Honshu, where it was customary for women to look

after horses. A rich man had a fine stable in which was kept a
particularly beautiful stallion. The man's daughter groomed it and
the other horses, and one day she stroked the stallion three times and
said she considered it to be so beautiful that if it were a man she
would like to marry it. At these words the stallion fell in love with
the young woman.

So great was its passion that it would neither eat nor drink and it
became ill. Its owner sent for diviners to discover the cause of this
illness, and when he was told his horse was sick for love of his
daughter his rage was intense. So angry was he that he had the horse
killed and then skinned. The skin was laid in the sun to dry and the
young woman whom the animal had loved so deeply went to it to
pray for the spirit of the stallion. Suddenly the skin arose and
enveloped the girl and carried her up into the sky. Not long afterwards,
from the area where the skin had been seen to disappear, showers of

black and white insects descended, lighting upon the mulberry bushes on the rich man's estate. These insects began to eat the leaves, and as they did so they gave out a fine thread. They were reputed to be the first silk worms, the black ones emanating from the horse and the white ones from the girl. It is also said that the girl's father became richer still through the union between the spirit of his horse and his daughter.

In China, from where the story must have originally come, there are other legends concerning the unnatural love between a girl and a horse and the beginning of sericulture. But there, the legends are just told as stories. In Japan this one is used as part of a ritual to recall departed spirits. There are ten known variants of the tale, differing little from each other. But in none of them is the association between silk, a horse and a young woman explained.

There is a tenuous connection between horses and silk in the early part of the *Nihongi*. When Amaterasu was in her 'sacred weaving hall' weaving the 'garments of the gods' (Uke-mochi's eyebrows had already produced silk worms by the time this happened and Amaterasu herself had founded sericulture by putting the silk worms in her mouth and reeling silk from them, and so one can assume she was weaving with silk) Susano made a hole in the roof of the hall and flung down one of the piebald colts, which he had already let loose in his sister's rice fields. So startled was the Sun goddess that she hurt herself with the shuttle she was using.

Tales of specific objects and places, too, echo down the years in legend. An account appears in Richard M. Dorson's *Folk Legends of Japan* of the rebuilding of the Motomachi Bridge in Miyazaki on the east coast of Kyushu as recently as 1927. It was rebuilt at speed with the aid of the army because another bridge across the same river, the Oyodo, was also being restored, an operation which of necessity took longer. Two soldiers were lost during the course of the building, which only took three weeks, and their bodies were never found. A proposal that the name of the bridge be changed to Engineer Bridge, out of respect for the military engineers who built it, was disregarded and the bridge continued to be called Motomachi. Later it was told that at night marching feet and a marching song could be heard on the bridge. So some local people erected a shrine to the god of Water at one end of the edifice where tablets in memory of the two soldiers were placed. The rebuilt bridge was swept away by flood water, as its predecessor had been, at the end of the Second World War; but one assumes the ghostly sounds heard before the shrine was put there were not heard again.

And so, finally, from Kyushu, the island to which Saint Francis Xavier first brought Christianity to Japan and where, so very long before, the Beloved Grandson, Ninigi, came to found the Imperial dynasty and where the first Emperor, Jimmu Tenno, is also believed to have been born, back to the main island of Honshu. The province of Izumo, where Susano and his successors held sway and to which the White Hare of Oki came and where the reteller of so much that is old, Lafcadio Hearn, had his first Japanese home is in Honshu – and on the island stand Kyoto, Kamakura, Tokyo and Yokohama. A tale which has been told to foreign visitors to Japan for at least eighty years is that, if the last sight of land, as one's ship leaves Yokohama is the cone of Mount Fuji, then one will return.

Mt Fuji, or Fujiyama, is 12,389 feet high. An earthquake is said to have created it. The last major eruption occurred in 1707.

FURTHER READING LIST

Anesaki, Masaharu. *The mythology of all races*; vol. 8, *Japanese*.
Harrap, London, 1932.

Aston, W.G. (trans.). *Nihongi*: chronicles of Japan from the
earliest times to A.D. 697. Translated from the original Chinese and
Japanese. First published as a supplement to the Transactions
and Proceedings of the Japan Society of London by Kegan Paul,
Trench, Trubner & Co. in 1896. Reprinted and published by
Allen and Unwin, London, 1956.

Bosworth, A.R. *The lovely world of Richi-San*. Gollancz, London, 1960.

Chamberlain, Basil H. (trans.). *Ko-ji-ki: records of ancient matters*.
Transactions of the Asiatic Society of Japan, vol. 10 Supplement.
Lane, Crawford & Co., Kelly & Co., Yokohama, 1883.

Davis, F. Hadland. *Myths and legends of Japan*. Harrap, London,
1913.

de Garis, F. (for H.S.K. Yamaguchi). *We Japanese*. Yokohama, 1934
and 1935.

Dorson R.M. *Folk legends of Japan*. Charles Tuttle, Rutland, Vermont,
and Tokyo, 1962.

Eliséev, S. *Asiatic mythology: the mythology of Japan*. Harrap,
London, 1932.

Hearn, Lafcadio. *Glimpses of unfamiliar Japan*. Houghton Mifflin,
Boston, 1894.
Out of the East. Houghton Mifflin, Boston, 1895.
Kokoro. Houghton Mifflin, Boston, 1896.
Kwaidan. Houghton Mifflin, Boston, 1904.
The romance of the Milky Way. Houghton Mifflin, Boston, 1905.
Japan: an attempt at interpretation. Macmillan, New York, 1920.
Shadowings. Little, Brown & Co., Boston, 1925.

Joly, H.L. *Legend in Japanese art*. The Bodley Head, London, 1908.

Kennedy, M. *A short history of Japan*. New American Library,
New York, 1964.

Latourette, K.S. *The History of Japan*. Macmillan, New York, 1953.

Lum, P. *Fabulous beasts*. Thames and Hudson, London, 1952.

McAlpine, Helen and William. *Japanese tales and legends*. Oxford
University Press, London, 1958.

Ozaki, Y.T. *The Japanese fairy book*. Constable, London, 1903.

Redesdale, Lord. *Tales of old Japan*. Macmillan, London, 1908.

Seki, Keigo (ed.). *Folktales of Japan* trans. R.J. Adams. Routledge &
Kegan Paul, London, 1963.

Smith, R.G. *Ancient tales and folklore of Japan*. A. & C. Black,
London, 1908.

Storry, R. *A History of modern Japan*. Penguin Books,
Harmondsworth. Revised edition 1967.

Webster, R.G. *Japan: from the old to the new*. S.W. Patridge & Co.,
1905.

ACKNOWLEDGMENTS

The Publishers gratefully acknowledge the following for permission to reproduce the illustrations indicated:

Colour plates

Edward Binet: 2, 3, 5, 12, 16, 18, 19, 22, 24 and jackets. Yves Coffin: 11, 22. Hamlyn Group (by Michael Holford): 15, 23, 48, 61, 109, 117, 120. Michael Holford Library: 6-7, 37, 64, 69, 88, 92. Kyoto City Government: 41. Joan Martin: 40.

Black and White

Bildarchiv Foto Marburg: 52 left, 125. J. Allan Cash: 17 top, 25, 51, 57, 116, 119, 121, 129. Yves Coffin: 12, 20 bottom left, 20 bottom right, 24 right, 27 left, 31, 47 left, 52 right, 53, 55, 66 right, 75, 87, 98-99, 114, 131. Giraudon: 59 top, 126. Hamlyn Group (by Michael Holford): 63, 73. Hamlyn Group Picture Library: 10. Kokusai Bunka Shinkokai: 79. Larousse: 13, 16, 20 top, 35, 50, 136. Mansell: 123. R. P. Martin: 17 bottom. Metropolitan Museum of Art: 104. Musée Guimet: 38. Museum f. Völkerkunde: 26, 29 left, 42-43, 47 right, 54, 59 bottom, 60, 66 left, 71, 84, 86, 94 top, 101, 105, 106-107, 111-112, 122, 130, 132-133. Popper Photos: 115. Rijksmuseum voor Volkenkunde: 128. M. Sakamoto: 21, 46. Seattle Art Museum: 32-34, 39 left, 70, 80, 97, 124. University of Pennsylvania: 24 left. Victoria and Albert Museum: endpapers, 27 right, 28, 29 right, 30, 39 right, 58, 62, 67, 76, 78, 81-83, 90-91, 94 bottom, 100, 102-103, 110, 118, 134. William Rockhill Nelson Gallery of Art, Kansas City: 74.

INDEX